Ripple Quick Start Guide

Get started with XRP and develop applications on Ripple's blockchain

Febin John James

BIRMINGHAM - MUMBAI

Ripple Quick Start Guide

Commissioning Editor: Pavan Ramchandani
Acquisition Editor: Siddharth Mandal
Content Development Editor: Smit Carvalho
Technical Editor: Ralph Rosario
Copy Editor: Safis Editing
Project Coordinator: Pragati Shukla
Proofreader: Safis Editing
Indexer: Rekha Nair
Graphics: Alishon Mendonsa
Production Coordinator: Nilesh Mohite

First published: December 2018

Production reference: 1281218

Published by Packt Publishing Ltd.
Livery Place
35 Livery Street
Birmingham
B3 2PB, UK.

ISBN 978-1-78953-219-7

www.packtpub.com

To my family, Fr. James Eapen, Mariamma James, and Jenin Thomas James, for always being there for me.
To Hacker Noon, for opening up a world of opportunities to me.

– Febin John James

`mapt.io`

Mapt is an online digital library that gives you full access to over 5,000 books and videos, as well as industry leading tools to help you plan your personal development and advance your career. For more information, please visit our website.

Why subscribe?

- Spend less time learning and more time coding with practical eBooks and Videos from over 4,000 industry professionals

- Improve your learning with Skill Plans built especially for you

- Get a free eBook or video every month

- Mapt is fully searchable

- Copy and paste, print, and bookmark content

Packt.com

Did you know that Packt offers eBook versions of every book published, with PDF and ePub files available? You can upgrade to the eBook version at `www.packt.com` and as a print book customer, you are entitled to a discount on the eBook copy. Get in touch with us at `customercare@packtpub.com` for more details.

At `www.packt.com`, you can also read a collection of free technical articles, sign up for a range of free newsletters, and receive exclusive discounts and offers on Packt books and eBooks.

Contributors

About the author

Febin John James is presently working on building autonomous lending and borrowing protocol on the Ethereum blockchain. He also works as a tech and marketing consultant to ICOs and blockchain-based start-ups. He has years of experience in building and scaling tech architectures from scratch. His blockchain stories on Medium have gained a lot of popularity and have been translated into multiple languages. He writes for well-known publications such as Hacker Noon and freeCodeCamp. He is also the author of the book, *Cloud is a Piece of Cake*. Previously, he worked as the CTO of Boutline, a sports start-up. He has also bagged devices, cash prizes, and recognition from companies such as Intel, Blackberry, and Microsoft.

I want to start by thanking David Smooke. A few years ago, he noticed my stories on Medium and added me to his publication, Hacker Noon. My viewership drastically increased overnight. This brought me great opportunities to work with people around the world. This book was the result of one such opportunity. Secondly, I want to thank Siddharth Mandal from Packt Publishing, who noticed my work and brought me the privilege of being a Packt author. I also want to thank Smit Carvalho and the Packt Publishing team, who have worked hard to release this book.

About the reviewer

Iqbal Singh, known as Chief Blockchain Architect, is the CEO and founder of Immanent Solutions, a management consulting and blockchain solutions firm based in Chandigarh, India. Iqbal possesses 15 years' extensive hands-on experience in blockchain, IT, IoT, AI, automation, and the RIA industry. Iqbal has been providing business solutions for Bitcoin, Ethereum, Ripple, and R3 Corda Blockchain. Heading 30 professional teams working in data science, algorithms, and cryptography (SHA256, X11, and Script), Blockchain, ICO, Coin, ERC20, Exchange, BTC, and ETH Expert Architect.

> *I personally recommend this book to all blockchain people to get a clear and precise understanding of Ripple. A highly recommended book!*

Packt is searching for authors like you

If you're interested in becoming an author for Packt, please visit authors.packtpub.com and apply today. We have worked with thousands of developers and tech professionals, just like you, to help them share their insight with the global tech community. You can make a general application, apply for a specific hot topic that we are recruiting an author for, or submit your own idea.

Table of Contents

Preface

Money has evolved over the years. In its early days, it was physical objects, eventually becoming gold. It later took the form of gold coins. Since these coins were expensive to mint, money later took the form of paper currency. The evolution of technology has given us digital currencies, though they still struggle to keep up with the pace of technology. This is because different banks have different systems that don't work effectively with each other. A lot of processes in these traditional systems are still manual. This has slowed down the movement of money between people and organizations. The security of these systems has also been proven weak on numerous occasions.

We need a system with strong interoperability and security features. In 2009, a decentralized currency called Bitcoin was invented with strong security, privacy, and autonomy features. It enables people to send money across borders without revealing their identity. The system is completely autonomous. It doesn't need any human supervision. Computers that run the Bitcoin program communicate with each other to enable global payments.

Later, Ethereum was invented. It is more than a payment network. It enables people to program money and build decentralized applications through smart contracts. Though Bitcoin and Ethereum are great innovations, they can only process a limited number of transactions per minute. The bigger problem being they don't support existing fiat currencies such as the US dollar or the euro.

Ripple provides a decentralized system that allows you to transfer anything of value. Though it issues its own currency, called XRP, it allows the transfer of fiat currencies and physical assets (as long as they can be represented digitally). It also provides a solution for banks that integrates with their traditional systems to make international transfers fast and cheap. Furthermore, it allows you to program the flow of money with its escrow, check, and payment channel features. Since it's an open system, it allows anyone anywhere in the world to build applications on top of it.

Who this book is for

This book is for beginners who want to understand and use Ripple's blockchain technology. If you are a trader who wants to work with XRP (Ripple's currency), this book will help you choose and set up a Ripple wallet and make money transfers. It will also help you to manage and protect your Ripple wallet. This book covers the basics of the blockchain, so no prior knowledge of blockchain is required. If you are an investor or a finance professional, you will gain an understanding of the applications of Ripple, which will help you gain insights into the future potential of this technology. This book also highlights common misconceptions about Ripple and its potential risks. If you are a developer, you will learn how to use the Ripple API to build applications on top of Ripple. Developers are assumed to have a basic background of JavaScript, HTML, and CSS.

What this book covers

Chapter 1, *Getting Started with Ripple,* In this chapter, we will start by learning the fundamentals of blockchain and cryptocurrencies. You will learn how and why blockchain was invented. We will discuss the challenges faced by early cryptocurrencies. Later, we will study how Ripple addresses those challenges. You will also learn how Ripple manages to make global payments fast and cheap, and we will look into the potential risks of Ripple.

Chapter 2, *Working with the Ripple Currency XRP,* In this chapter, we will take a hands-on approach to work with XRP. We will learn how to set up a Ripple wallet, and see how seamlessly you can transfer money to a friend abroad. We will discuss the different kind of wallets you can use to store XRP. We will also discuss the security precautions you need to take to keep your money safe.

Chapter 3, *Applications of Ripple*, In this chapter, we will understand the applications of Ripple. We will learn how Ripple's xCurrent software integrates with traditional systems to make cross-border transactions efficient. We will also learn how Ripple enables its users to make cross-currency payments. We will then study the check, escrow, and payment channel offerings of Ripple, and learn about its Initial Coin Offering and the fully functional decentralized exchange inside Ripple.

Chapter 4, *Getting Started with the Ripple API*, In this chapter, we will learn how to work with the Ripple API. We will set up the development environment and connect to the test network to send money from a Ripple account. We will also learn how to build web applications using the Ripple API. If you have never worked on a blockchain-based system, this chapter will give you a kickstart.

`Chapter 5`, *Developing Applications Using the Ripple API*, In this chapter, you will learn how to use advanced offerings of Ripple, such as checks and escrows. You will learn how to send checks, cash checks, and create and release escrows. We will also integrate the Ripple API to build web applications. These applications will allow non-developers to easily use the check and escrow features of Ripple.

To get the most out of this book

If you are a developer who wants to build applications on top of Ripple, you need to have basic knowledge of HTML, CSS, and JavaScript.

Download the example code files

You can download the example code files for this book from your account at `www.packt.com`. If you purchased this book elsewhere, you can visit `www.packt.com/support` and register to have the files emailed directly to you.

You can download the code files by following these steps:

1. Log in or register at `www.packt.com`.
2. Select the **SUPPORT** tab.
3. Click on **Code Downloads & Errata**.
4. Enter the name of the book in the **Search** box and follow the onscreen instructions.

Once the file is downloaded, please make sure that you unzip or extract the folder using the latest version of:

- WinRAR/7-Zip for Windows
- Zipeg/iZip/UnRarX for Mac
- 7-Zip/PeaZip for Linux

The code bundle for the book is also hosted on GitHub at `https://github.com/PacktPublishing/Ripple-Quick-Start-Guide`. In case there's an update to the code, it will be updated on the existing GitHub repository.

We also have other code bundles from our rich catalog of books and videos available at `https://github.com/PacktPublishing/`. Check them out!

Conventions used

There are a number of text conventions used throughout this book.

`CodeInText`: Indicates code words in text, database table names, folder names, filenames, file extensions, pathnames, dummy URLs, user input, and Twitter handles. Here is an example: "Mount the downloaded `WebStorm-10*.dmg` disk image file as another disk in your system."

A block of code is set as follows:

```
{
    "Account": "rfkE1aSy9G8Upk4JssnwBxhEv5p4mn2KTy",
    "TransactionType": "CheckCash",
    "Amount": "50000000",
    "CheckID":
"838766BA2B995C00744175F69A1B11E32C3DBC40E64801A4056FCBD657F57334",
    "Fee": "12"
}
```

Bold: Indicates a new term, an important word, or words that you see onscreen. For example, words in menus or dialog boxes appear in the text like this. Here is an example: "Select **System info** from the **Administration** panel."

Warnings or important notes appear like this.

Tips and tricks appear like this.

Get in touch

Feedback from our readers is always welcome.

General feedback: If you have questions about any aspect of this book, mention the book title in the subject of your message and email us at `customercare@packtpub.com`.

Errata: Although we have taken every care to ensure the accuracy of our content, mistakes do happen. If you have found a mistake in this book, we would be grateful if you would report this to us. Please visit www.packt.com/submit-errata, selecting your book, clicking on the Errata Submission Form link, and entering the details.

Piracy: If you come across any illegal copies of our works in any form on the Internet, we would be grateful if you would provide us with the location address or website name. Please contact us at copyright@packt.com with a link to the material.

If you are interested in becoming an author: If there is a topic that you have expertise in and you are interested in either writing or contributing to a book, please visit authors.packtpub.com.

Reviews

Please leave a review. Once you have read and used this book, why not leave a review on the site that you purchased it from? Potential readers can then see and use your unbiased opinion to make purchase decisions, we at Packt can understand what you think about our products, and our authors can see your feedback on their book. Thank you!

For more information about Packt, please visit packt.com.

Getting Started with Ripple
1

Money has undergone evolution since its existence: from a barter system to physical objects to gold coins. Paper currency replaced gold coins, which was again replaced, to an extent, by digital money. Even before digital money replaces paper currencies, we can start seeing money taking a new form through cryptocurrencies. Bitcoin was the first decentralized cryptocurrency. Later, many cryptocurrencies such as LiteCoin, Ethereum, and Ripple were introduced to the market.

In this chapter, we will be exploring the following topics to understand the basics of Ripple and why it is necessary:

- Introduction to the blockchain, the underlying technology behind cryptocurrencies
- Introduction to Bitcoin, the first decentralized cryptocurrency
- Inefficiencies with traditional payment systems
- Introduction to Ripple, the currency agnostic cryptocurrency
- The functionality of the Ripple Protocol
- Key features of Ripple
- Potential risks of Ripple

The need for decentralization

Few diamond firms found it unusual when Punjab National Bank demanded 100% cash margins for issuing **LOUs (letters of undertaking)**, which is a form of bank guarantee under which its customers can raise money from any other Indian bank's foreign branch in the form of short-term credit.

However, the firms argued that this requirement was not enforced for the LOUs they received since 2010. This raised alarms and PNB called for an investigation. They found out a few employees had been issuing fake LOUs through the SWIFT system (a messaging system between banks). Unfortunately, the software that PNB used to facilitate SWIFT didn't record its transactions. This allowed the fraud to go undetected. A month later, PNB found out that the scam cost them $1.8 billion.

We have been using centralized systems to build internet applications for a long time. Here, business logic and data lies in one or more central servers. Client applications communicate with these servers to process information. Bank employees use software, which interfaces with the bank's central system, to facilitate transactions. Another example is your bank's application: when you tap to send money, the request is sent to the bank's centralized system for processing.

What happens if that central system is compromised? What happens when someone makes a transaction and deletes its traces? How do we prevent such fraudulent activities?

To solve these problems, we need to satisfy the following requirements:

- A system shouldn't have a central point of attack
- Transactions or data in the system must be tamper-proof

These are the key concepts behind distributed ledger systems or blockchain-based systems. Technically, these concepts are known as *decentralization* and *immutability*.

Introduction to blockchain

The word blockchain itself is descriptive. Here, blocks of digital information are linked back to one another like a chain of blocks. In the following image, we can see blocks that contain a series of transactions:

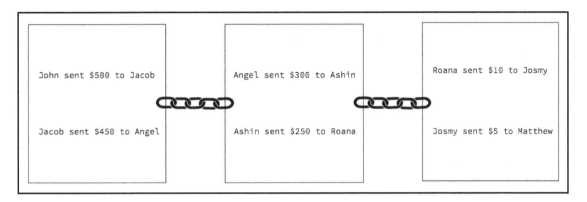

If someone tampers with the first transaction of the second block by altering $300 to $3,000, Ashin's balance would have an additional $2,700. Such tampering would lead to disastrous consequences. Hence, blockchain uses cryptography to make itself tamper-proof.

In the following blocks, we have added an additional attribute, the hash:

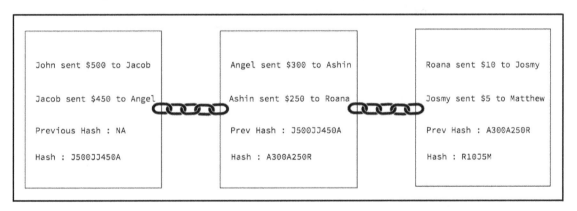

A hash is a set of characters that represents the contents of the block. It's calculated using a cryptographic hash function. For the sake of simplicity, we have made a simple hash by taking the first letters from the names of senders and beneficiaries. We also added the amount transferred in the middle of those first letters, and hence the hash for the first block is **J500JJ450A**. (*Technically, this is not how a hash function works, but you get the idea.*)

Since the first block has no preceding block, its previous hash field is not applicable. However, from the second block, all successive blocks have stored the hash of its previous block.

If someone tries to tamper with the first block and change John's transfer from $500 to $5,000, the hash of that block changes from **J500JJ450A** to **J5000JJ450A**. However, the successive block has already stored the hash as **J500JJ450A**. This mismatch would break the chain. Hence, the purpose of the hash is to ensure that blocks are not tampered with.

What if someone tries to change a block and the hash of all the succeeding blocks?

Different blockchains have different mechanisms to protect themselves from such situations. In the Bitcoin system, before a block is added to the chain, certain computationally intense tasks must be carried out.

Blocks are only confirmed once proof of running such intensive tasks or proof-of-work is shown. Hence, if a hacker wants to modify the hashes of n blocks, they need to run such computationally intense tasks n times to show the proof-of-work. Considering the present limits in computation, this scenario are highly unlikely.

Secondly, blockchain systems are decentralized. This means that a blockchain program isn't executed by a single computer, but all the computers in its network work collectively in executing its instructions. The data in the blockchain is also replicated in all the computers present in the network. Hence, the system would consider only what the majority say is correct.

Introduction to Bitcoin

Blockchain's application lies beyond building tamper-proof records. It can be used to make autonomous and automated systems that can work without human intervention. Bitcoin is an automated system that allows for the transfer of cryptoassets (bitcoin), directly between users without any intermediaries.

There are no signup forms to create a wallet. Instead, user keys are generated using cryptography. Here, there are two keys: the public key and the private key. The public key is like a username and the private key is similar to a password. These keys look like a long string with a combination of letters and numbers (for example, `18XgQU8FJbi8Vje6658hUKjeKjbbDS6eDa`).

Privacy is one of the key features of Bitcoin. Since no user information is provided to the Bitcoin system, the system doesn't know any details about its users. Unless users expose their public key, they remain anonymous.

If a user wants to send money to another user, the sender needs to create a message, sign it and broadcast it. The broadcast message is later verified and committed to the ledger.

The following image depicts how a transaction makes its way to Bitcoin's tamper-proof ledger:

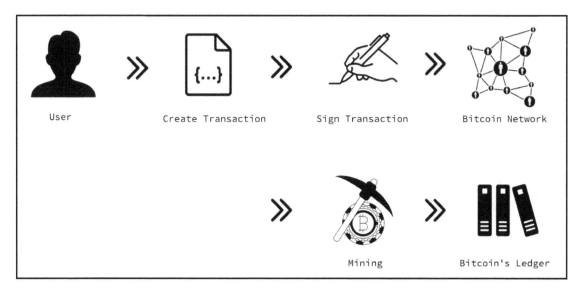

If Sosha wants to send 5 Bitcoin to Sneha, the message would look like the following:

Message: *I am sending 5 Bitcoin to Sneha*
Signature: Sosha's signature
Public Key: Sosha's public key

The signature is generated using a cryptographic function that takes Sosha's public key, private key, and message as input. Then, it generates the signature as output.

Now, anyone on the bitcoin network can verify it with another `crypto` function, which takes the public key, signature, and message as input. If the message is modified, the cryptographic function will throw an error.

Every 10 minutes, the bitcoin network groups new transactions as a block. This new block is only added to the blockchain once it is mined. To mine the block, the system creates a computational puzzle that should be solved by the miners. Here, humans don't solve the puzzles; instead, mining devices do.

Miners compete to solve this puzzle, and the first miner who solves this puzzle is rewarded with x number of Bitcoins. Presently, the reward is around 12.5 Bitcoin. These coins are minted out of thin air, and this is how new coins are added to the system.

Once a block is mined, it is permanently added to the blockchain. These blocks of transactions are visible to anyone. This results in transparency that, in turn, results in trust. Anyone can look up any blocks on the blockchain and also the transaction that occurred in the block. Here's the summary of block #**544473**:

SUMMARY OF BLOCK #544473	
Number Of Transactions	1698
Block Reward	12.5 BTC
Nonce	581029573
Output Total	6,816.92167998 BTC
Estimated Transaction Volume	569.44698504 BTC
Transaction Fees	0.0539869 BTC
Height	544473
Timestamp	2018-10-05 08:17:54
Received Time	2018-10-05 08:17:54
Relayed By	BTC.com
Difficulty	7,454,968,648,263.24
Bits	388350353
Size	1038.251 kB
Weight	3601.022 kWU
Version	0x20000000
Hash	0000000000000000000ed31c99bd128cab170d78303c086a2c91968af6b7024a
Previous Block	00000000000000000000061335a0841bd97967bae63d5d20d599fe7cb4d0708790

Censorship resistance is a key feature of this innovation. Since there are no central servers, governments cannot enforce a ban on the system. To prevent bitcoin systems from functioning, all of its users' computers must be shut down. Since there are millions of such nodes in the network, it is almost impossible to achieve this.

Inefficiencies in payment systems

Speed and cost is an important factor in any payment system. In traditional banking, system money needs to move through several intermediaries before it reaches its destination. Each of these intermediaries adds to the transaction fees. Settlement happens slowly, since manual work is involved.

Consider John, who's a US account holder and wants to send money to his friend, Peter, in Germany. Here's how the money would flow from John's bank account to Peter's account:

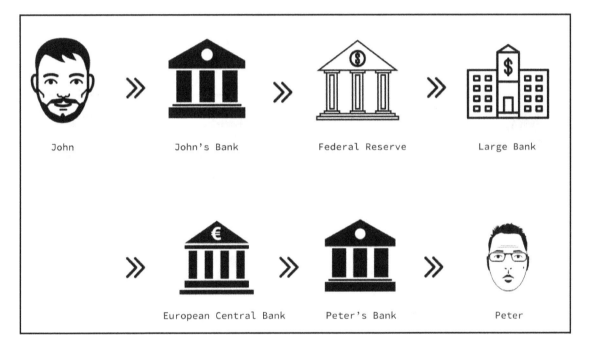

Here is how the transfer happens:

1. John places a request to transfer money.
2. John's bank is a small bank and doesn't have an EU banking license. Hence, it needs the help of a large US bank to make the transfer. It sends money to the bank, which possesses an EU banking license.
3. However, the small bank cannot transfer funds directly to the large bank; it has to route funds through a federal reserve.

4. Once the money reaches the large bank, it transfers money from its nostro account to Peter's bank.

5. However, the transfer doesn't happen directly, since the funds need to be routed through the European Central Bank.

Each of these intermediates adds to the transaction fee. If $5,000 needs to be transferred, around $250 is charged as transaction fees.

International money transfer through Bitcoin

Let's understand how international transfer can be simplified using Bitcoin.

Here's how the money would flow from John's bank account to Peter's account:

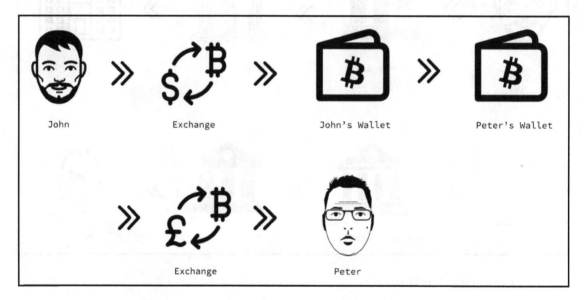

Here's how international money transfer happens through Bitcoin:

1. John exchanges his USD for Bitcoin
2. He directly transfers Bitcoin to Peter's account without any intermediaries
3. Peter exchanges his Bitcoin for Euros

Disadvantages of Bitcoin

Though this process reduces intermediaries and reduces the transfer time to almost 60 minutes, it brings in new issues. Let's take a look at the disadvantages of Bitcoin:

- Bitcoin's system doesn't plug in to existing banking systems or currencies
- Users need to create bitcoin wallets and exchange it with their native currency
- Its market prices are highly volatile
- Bitcoin is not widely accepted as a currency; in certain countries, it's illegal
- It could handle only a limited number of transactions per second
- Its transaction fees are high
- Its proof-of-work mechanism demands an immense amount of energy

The key disadvantage of Bitcoin is that it doesn't work with existing currencies and forces the user to make transactions in Bitcoin. Since the currency is not widely accepted and some countries have banned transacting in Bitcoin, it brings in new risks to its users.

Ripple

Ripple addressed these issues and came up with a solution to incorporate blockchain with existing currencies. Ripple is a blockchain-based payment system that makes the global transfer of money cheaper, faster, and more efficient. Here, money doesn't need to be fiat currencies, but any item of value (for example, gold, digital assets, etc). It also issues its own native currency called XRP.

International money transfer through Ripple

Here's how money moves across borders through the Ripple protocol:

1. John's bank would use Ripple's system to initiate the USD to EUR exchange. Market makers will compete by posting bids.
2. Ripple's system is optimized to select the cheapest offer. The market maker will buy USD from John's bank and Ripple will transfer Euros from the market maker to Peter's account. These transactions are atomic, which means that both of these transactions happen simultaneously or they don't happen at all.

The following image depicts the flow of money from John's bank account to Peter's bank account through **The Ripple Protocol**:

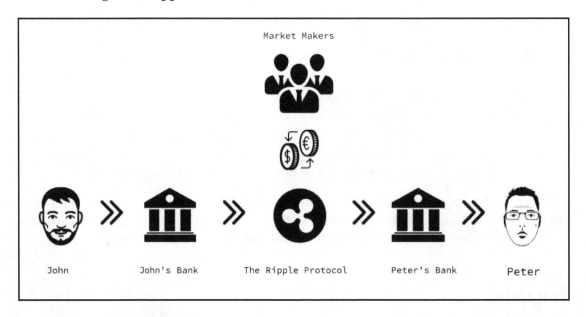

Ripple reduces transfer time from days to a few seconds. This is because the transfer happens without intermediaries and the settlement process requires no human intervention. The average transaction fee in Ripple is around $0.0006; that's a significant reduction of cost.

The important point to note here is that users need not exchange Ripples. Ripple can be seamlessly plugged into a banks' systems. Hence, end users such as John and Peter don't have to interact with Ripple's blockchain. Now, let's go deep into the Ripple protocol and study how it works.

The Ripple Protocol

We will start by studying the details of how accounts are created, funded, and managed. Please note that in this chapter, we will only understand the underlying process of account creation, sending money, and so on. In the next chapter, we will learn to do it practically using tools that do these process by the click of a button.

Account creation

Similar to the Bitcoin system, Ripple has no signup process. Instead, we need to generate key pairs using cryptography. Since the process is mathematical, it can be done offline.

We start by generating a seed. A seed is a set of random characters. For the sake of simplicity, let's consider the seed as A34939449DJMABESEHLODAER. Once the seed is generated, a cryptographic function is used to derive a public key from it. We will use a simple function for the sake of understanding. Our function derives the public key from the seed by taking the first sixteen characters of the seed, A34939449DJMABES.

This is a one-way process: a public key cannot be used to derive the seed. Later, we can derive our Ripple identification by using the cryptographic hash function. This is the address we mention when we want to receive payments. This is done by creating the hash of the hash of the public key.

We will again use a simple function for the sake of understanding. We will strip the first eight characters to generate the first hash, A3493944. Then, we will strip the first four characters of the first hash to create the second hash, A349.

Now, A349 is our identity on the Ripple network. The key point to note here is that if you lose your seed, your account is compromised, since every other key can be derived from it. The following image demonstrates how the seed phrase is used to derive the public key and the Ripple identity:

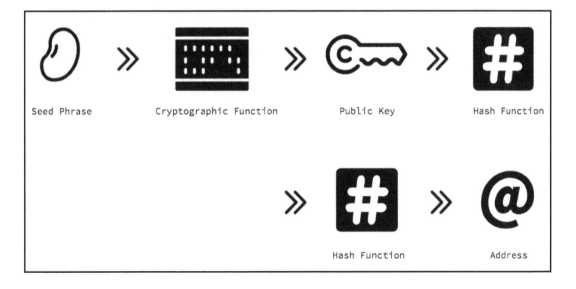

This is a how a seed, public key, and account ID actually looks:

```
{
 "seed": "sstV9YX8k7yTRzdkRFAHmX7EVqMfX",
 "public_key": "aBQXEw1vZD3geCX3rHL8qy8ooDomdFuxZcWrbRZKZjdDkUoUjGVS",
 "account_id": "rDGnaDqJczDAjwKHKdhGRJh2G7zJfZhj5q"
}
```

Reserve

Generating key pairs doesn't create an account in the XRP ledger. To prevent Ripple's ledger from growing excessively large, new accounts must be funded with a reserve amount of XRP from an existing amount to make them functional. The present reserve amount required is 20 XRP.

You can buy Ripple from a private exchange and send it to your Ripple's account ID. This transaction will create your account in the Ripple ledger. Now, your account will become functional and you can make transactions on Ripple. However, the reserve amount will remain locked.

The important point to note here is that funding an account doesn't give you access to an account. Only the person holding the secret key has access to its funds. It's possible to fund an address that doesn't have a secret key. However, this would result in a permanent loss of the sent XRP.

A Ripple account also has additional attributes such as a sequence number and history of transactions. The sequence number starts at 1, and every time a transaction is made it increases. It also holds the transaction history on how they affected the account's balances. The following image shows the front end of a simple ripple wallet:

Balances of a Ripple Account. Source: `http://xrpcharts.ripple.com`.

Transactions

In order to send money, we need to create, sign, and submit the transaction to Ripple servers.

The following image depicts how a transaction makes its way to Ripple's tamper-proof ledger:

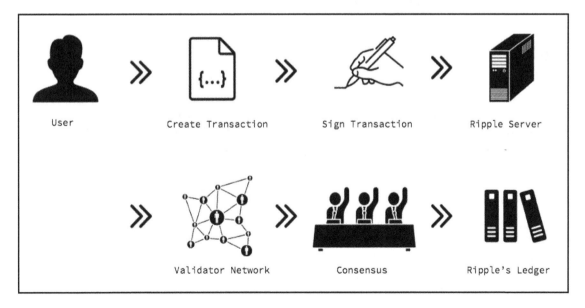

We would start by creating a transaction JSON. Here's an example of a transaction in JSON format. It includes sender address, destination address, currency type, amount to be transferred, and so on:

```
{
  "TransactionType" : "Payment",
   "Account" : "rf1BiGeXwwQoi4Z2ueFYTEXSwuJYfV2Jpn",
   "Destination" : "ra5nK24KXfn9AHvsdFTKHSANinZseWnPcX",
   "Amount" :
     {
        "currency" : "USD",
        "value" : "2",
        "issuer" : "rf1BiseXwwQoi8Z2ueFYTEXSwuJYfV2Jpn"
     },
   "Fee": "10",
   "Flags": 2147482648,
   "Sequence": 3,
}
```

We authorize the transaction using our secret key. Later, we submit it to the Ripple server for validation. Once it validates the transaction, it conveys the transaction to fellow members of the network. They apply these transactions to their version of the ledger in canonical order and submit the results. If enough validators reach consensus by sharing the same ledger, the transaction is confirmed and permanently added to the blockchain. If the transaction fails, it's also included in the ledgers. This is because failed transactions burn XRP and modify the account balances. XRP is burnt to prevent spammers from attacking the network with failed transactions.

Multisigning

We can add additional security to our account by authorizing transactions with a combination of multiple secret keys. We can put a requirement that multiple people need to sign the transaction for it to be valid. If we add Bob, Alice, and Ruth in the signer list and if Bob's account is compromised, the account is still safe, since transactions signed only by Bob are now invalid.

Consensus

Bitcoin uses the proof-of-work mechanism to prevent malicious users from spending Bitcoins they don't have. However, its mechanism is costly and slow since it uses an immense amount of energy. Ripple came up with a consensus mechanism that is cheaper and faster.

In order to validate a transaction, Ripple doesn't rely on central authority. Instead, it has made a set of rules that the nodes in the network must follow to agree and reach on a consensus on what must go on the permanent ledger. This set of rules are called the consensus protocol.

Important properties of the consensus protocol

The following are the properties of Ripple's consensus protocol:

- Every participant who uses the XRP ledger should agree on which transaction occurred in what order and what the resulting state is (an account balance is an example for the resulting state).
- A central authority is not required to confirm and validate transactions.
- The system will continue to validate transaction even if its people in the network decided to join, leave, or act maliciously.
- If a lot of people in the network misbehave, the network will stop making progress. This is to ensure correctness in the ledger.
- Unlike other blockchain-based currencies, confirming transactions in the ledger does not require people to waste energy.

Ledger versions

Similar to Bitcoin, XRP also processes transactions in blocks. These blocks are called ledger versions. They contain three components:

1. **State data**: This contains values such as current account balance and other objects stored in the ledger. For example, Bob's Account Balance: 5 XRP, Alice's Account Balance: 10 XRP.
2. **Newly applied transactions**: These are the set of transactions that were applied to the previous ledger and hence resulted in the current state (Bob sent $5 USD to Alice, Alice sent 30 XRP to Bob).
3. **Metadata**: This contains information about the ledger and the preceding parent ledger. It includes values such as the ledger index and the cryptographic hash.

Validation

In the Ripple network, the participant can choose its list of validators. This list is called the Unique Node List. When a transaction reaches these validators, they take the previously confirmed or the validated ledger version as the starting point. Then they apply new transactions in the canonical order and share their results.

Here's an example of a confirmed block. Validators would use this as a starting point:

Confirmed Block No	5
Transaction 1	Alice Sent Bob $5
Transaction 2	Bob sent Peter $20
State	Alice has $20, Bob has $30

Here comes a new set of transactions to be validated:

Alice Sent Bob $5	24 Sep 2018 09:12:17
Bob sent Peter $20	24 Sep 2018 10:12:17

If these transactions are applied according to in the order of their timestamp, the resulting state would be as follows:

State	Alice has $15, Bob has $15

The validators should arrive at the preceding conclusion. If they don't agree, then they would modify their proposal to match the validators they trust. This would continue in multiple rounds until they reach consensus. If 80% of the validators reach an agreement, then the transactions are confirmed and permanently added to the ledger. Otherwise, the ledger would stop making progress.

Advantages of Ripple

Now, let's have a look at key advantages of the Ripple cryptocurrency. These are the features that make it stand out among the other competitive currencies in the market.

Currency agnostic

Though the Ripple protocol has a native currency, XRP, it's not mandatory for users to transact only in XRP. It can transfer any item of value (fiat currencies, digital assets, and so on).

Simplified consensus

Unlike Bitcoin, Ripple has a simplified consensus or settlement mechanism. Once a transaction is signed and broadcasted, a selected number of Ripple servers reach a consensus on whether the transaction is valid or not. This process happens in 6 to 10 seconds. It can process around 1500 transactions per second; this is drastically higher than Bitcoin.

Low fee

Due to the simplified consensus mechanism and automated settlement, Ripple drastically reduces the transaction fee.

Reduced foreign exchange cost

The Ripple system is designed to select the cheapest bidder. This forces the market maker to make bids at competitive prices.

Pathfinding algorithm

Due to market limits, certain currencies cannot be exchanged directly. EUR/KRW is an example of such a currency that doesn't have a tight market. Hence, EUR needs to be exchanged for USD and USD needs to be exchanged for JPY and, finally, JPY can be exchanged for KRW. Ripple's system has a built-in pathfinding algorithm that would make the exchange by searching for the cheapest possible path.

Adaptable cryptography

Though the Ripple systems rely on time-tested encryptions such as ECDSA, it is also extendible to modern algorithms such as Ed25519. The system has the capability to add or disable algorithms. This is a great security feature, since if an encryption mechanism becomes obsolete, it can be replaced with a new one.

Anti-spam mechanism

In order to prevent spam requests on Ripple's ledger, while sending transactions a small amount of XRP must be destroyed. This fee is negligible for legitimate users, but can be costly for spammers who are trying to attack the network with bulk transactions.

Potential risks of Ripple

Now, let's look at the potential risks of Ripple. These are the few challenges Ripple would face to kick off as a currency.

1. Regulatory issues
2. Trust issues
3. Security vulnerabilities
4. Problems of being an open protocol

Regulatory issues

Certain countries such as India have banned cryptocurrencies and in certain countries laws on digital currencies are unclear. On the Ripple network, users are allowed to be anonymous. However, most governments are likely to have a problem with it.

Though governments cannot disable the XRP ledger, they can restrict people from buying XRP using fiat currencies such as USD and INR. In India, RBI has banned people from using credit cards to buy Bitcoins.

There are a lot of cryptocurrencies in the market with Ripple. Some of them are legitimate, some are scams. However, it would take time for the governments to understand the potential of cryptocurrencies. They would have a much harder time to distinguish the legitimate ones. Hence, it is hard to predict how the future of cryptocurrency will shape out.

Trust Issues

Ripple allows its users to transfer anything of value. This is accomplished with the help of issuers who link their assets to the XRP ledger. When users transact on the Ripple network, they have the option to trust these issuers.

However, if issuers misbehave and claim to have assets they don't have on the XRP ledger, it would lead to big problems. The issued currencies owned by users would lose their value overnight. This can affect people's trust in the Ripple network.

Security vulnerabilities

Security bugs are common in most online systems. However, a loophole in a distributed ledger can be fatal, since it can cause irreversible damage as data once confirmed is final and no one can alter it.

In Ethereum, bad coding has led to a loss of millions of dollars. Since Ripple limits the functionality on which a user can build on top of, there would be less room for vulnerabilities.

The question is, can Ripple continue to evolve without having any major security bugs?

Problems of being an open protocol

Ripple's code is totally free and open source. The problem with open protocols is that they can be forked easily. Bitcoin protocol was forked multiple times to create other currencies such as Bitcoin Cash and LiteCoin.

People can easily fork Ripple's code and build an advanced protocol that can compete with Ripple. Hence, partnerships are the key to Ripple's future. They need more financial institutions using the XRP ledger.

Summary

In this chapter, we learned the answers to the following questions.

- Why was decentralization necessary?
- What is blockchain?
- What is Bitcoin?
- What are the disadvantages of Bitcoin?
- What is Ripple?
- How does Ripple make international money transfers efficient?
- How does Ripple work?
- What are the key features of Ripple?
- What are the potential risks of Ripple?

Now that we understand how ripple works in theory, we will learn how to do some real transactions on Ripple's ledger in the next chapter.

Working with Ripple Currency XRP

2

In the previous chapter, we learned how Ripple works in theory. In this chapter, we will take a hands-on approach and learn to work with Ripple currency. You need to use a Ripple wallet to buy, hold, and transfer Ripples. There are different kinds of Ripple wallets, so you need to choose one that fits your requirements. In this chapter, you will learn to choose a wallet and use it to buy and transfer Ripples. We'll also go through security measures to keep your Ripples safe.

In this chapter, we will cover the following topics:

- Types of Ripple wallets
- Learning to choose your wallet
- Setting up a Ripple account
- Activating the Ripple account
- Making an international transfer
- Trading XRP
- Importing an existing wallet
- Setting up an offline wallet
- Protecting your Ripples

Types of wallets

Our physical wallets hold cash, identity cards, credit cards, and so on. Similarly, cryptocurrency wallets hold our public/private keys. They also help you check your account balance, see previous transactions, and assist you in sending and receiving money. You will need to select the wallet that best suits your needs.

 If you have skipped the previous chapter, think of the public key as the username and the private key as a password.

Online wallets

A beginner will find online wallets easy to use. It's similar to using an online bank account. Here, you don't have access to your private key because it is maintained by the online wallet provider. Secret keys that are stored online are known as hot wallets.

You can log in to online wallets using a browser or a mobile app. You can check your balance, send or receive money, and see your past transactions. Though these wallets are easy to use, they are prone to attacks. If their systems are breached, the private keys of users can be stolen. Such incidents have happened in the past. `Coinpayments` and `Gatehub.net` are examples of online wallets.

Desktop/mobile wallets

In a desktop/mobile wallet, the public and private key pairs are stored on your desktop/mobile device. The benefit here is that you have complete control over your wallet. However, if you lose or erase your devices, you cannot retrieve your wallet.

These wallets will allow you to check your balance, see past transactions, and help you with sending and receiving money. They often allow you to take a backup of your wallet. If you have a backup, you can restore your wallet, even when your device is erased or lost. Though these wallets are safer than online wallets, they are prone to virus attacks. Toast wallet is an example of a desktop/mobile wallet.

Offline wallets

An offline wallet doesn't store your public/private keys. It will help you to generate your keys and log in to your wallet without connecting to the internet (you will need internet access to submit signed transactions, though).

They allow you to send or receive money, see your balance, and view past transactions. You are responsible for keeping your private key safe. If you lose your private key, there is no way to recover your wallet. `Exarpy` is an example of an offline wallet.

Hardware wallets

In a hardware wallet, your private key is stored in a hardware device. It is securely stored and cannot be copied from the device, and so it is safe from viruses. You can plug hardware wallets into your USB port and use its software to check your balance, view past transactions, and send or receive money. `Trezor` is an example of a hardware wallet.

Paper wallets

A paper wallet is made by printing keys that are generated by an offline paper wallet generator. Since the keys are not stored online, they are known as cold wallets. They are mostly used for one-time redemption. Though they are highly secure when compared to other wallets, they are prone to physical damage and theft.

How do I choose my wallet?

If you are getting started and want to get the hang of cryptocurrencies, use an online wallet. However, do not use it to store crypto assets of a higher value.

If you are comfortable using desktop and mobile apps and not highly concerned about security, you can go with desktop/mobile wallets. Remember, your wallet is prone to virus attacks.

If you are highly concerned about security but need assistance to manage your keys, go for a hardware wallet.

If you are a pro and can manage the keys on your own, you can go for an offline/paper wallet.

Setting up a Ripple account

We'll be using Toast wallet (a desktop/mobile wallet) to set up our Ripple account. You can download the app on your desktop or mobile. You can choose any other wallet of your choice—the onboarding process won't be exactly the same, but similar.

The first time you open Toast wallet, you'll be shown the license agreement. Scroll down and you will see the **Create a New Wallet** button, as shown in the following screenshot on the left. Once you click on this button, you will be asked to set a six-digit pin, as in the following screenshot on the right. This is to prevent your wallet from unauthorized usage. Every time you open your wallet, you need to provide the six-digit pin to gain access to your wallet:

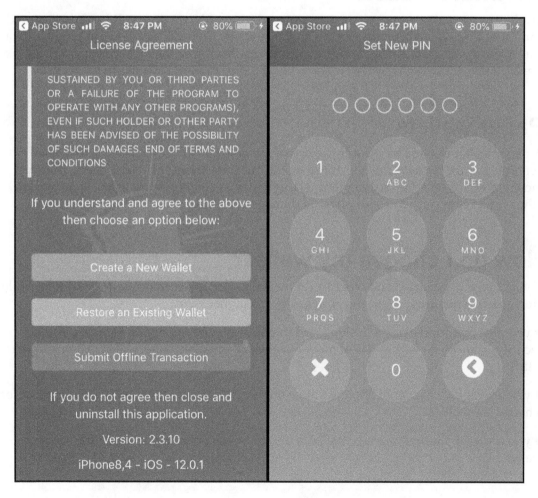

You will be then asked to set a passphrase, like in the following screenshot on the left. You need to provide the passphrase for sending XRP, importing an externally generated account, changing your pin, and so on. Once you set your passphrase, you will be asked to write down your recovery passphrase. If you forget it, you will lose access to the Toast wallet unless you can provide the recovery passphrase. Make sure you write it down.

If you lose your recovery passphrase, then there is no way to regain access to your account. This is because the Toast wallet doesn't store any of your account data online and hence cannot provide you with recovery assistance. Once you have noted down the recovery passphrase, press the **Finish Setup** button, as shown in the following screenshot on the right:

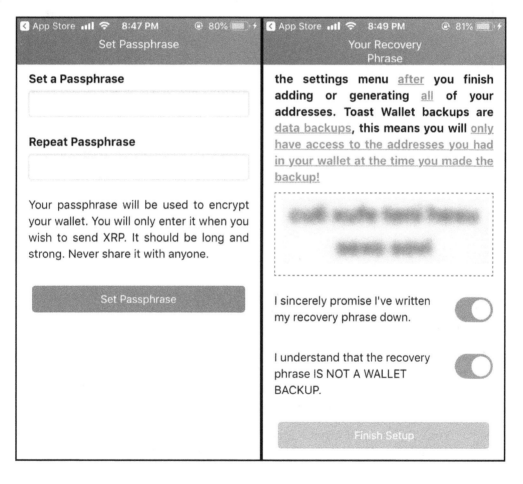

You are halfway through—you have set up your Toast wallet, but you haven't set up a Ripple account yet. Click on the + icon on the screen, as shown in the following screenshot on the left. Now, you will be taken to another screen (the right-hand side screenshot) where you are given the option to generate a new address:

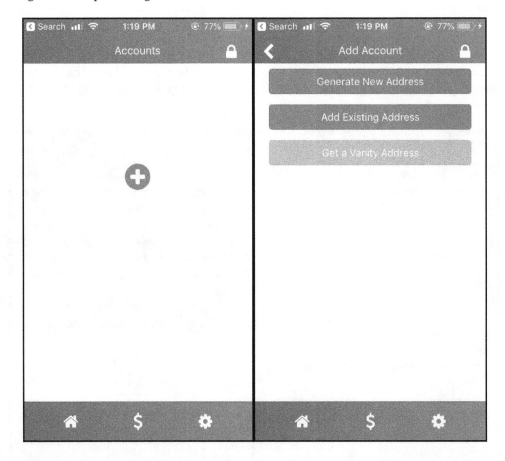

Tap the **Generate New Address** option, and you will be taken to another screen that asks you to provide a nickname for the account. Nicknames help you easily identify your accounts. You also need to provide your passphrase. Then, tap on **Import This Address**. You are asked to make a backup of your newly generated Ripple account.

Your Toast wallet is not a Ripple account. It's a tool that helps you create and manage Ripple accounts. The recovery passphrase you noted earlier was to help you gain access to your Toast wallet if you lose your passphrase.

However, let's imagine a scenario where you've lost your phone. You will want to migrate the Ripple account on your previous wallet to your new phone. This will be only possible if you have taken a backup of your wallet. Hence, it's important to note that the recovery passphrase and backup are two different things. You need to make sure that you note down both of these things when you want to make a recovery after your device is lost.

When you are prompted to make a backup, tap on the **Create a Backup Now** button. You will be shown your backup code. Please copy the backup code and store it somewhere safe. Also, note that you need to make a new backup when you change the pin or passphrase. Once you have made a note of your backup code, tap on the home button on the bottom of the screen. You will be able to see your account listed on the home screen.

Congratulations! You've successfully created your first Ripple account. Now, tap on the account's nickname. The long string on your phone's screen below your account's nickname is your public address. When you want to receive funds on your account, you give this address. You can tap the copy button toward the right-hand side of the public identity to copy the full address to your clipboard. The nickname is set only for your reference; it cannot be used as an identity:

Toast wallet gives you complete access to your wallet. In the preceding screenshot, you can also see the **Show Secret** button. This gives you access to your private key. You can now use this key to manage your Ripple account in other Ripple-supported wallets. You just have to import your secret key on those wallets.

Activating the Ripple account

The Ripple wallet you just set up is not ready to make transactions yet. To avoid spam, Ripple has made it necessary for all wallets to be funded with a fixed amount. Presently, this amount is 20 XRP. Hence, to activate your wallet, you need to send 20 XRP to your newly created Ripple account. Once your wallet has been funded with 20 XRP, it will be automatically activated.

There are multiple ways to buy XRP. For one, you can buy it from crypto exchanges such as Binance, CEX, and Bitfinex. However, most of these centralized exchanges require you to do KYC(Know Your Customer) verifications. Changelly (https://changelly.com/) allows you to buy XRP without verification, and their exchange process is seamless. Navigate to www.changelly.com and create an account there. Then, go back to the home screen.

If you have any other crypto assets such as Bitcoin or Ethereum, you can exchange them for XRP. If you don't have any crypto assets, you will need to spend a minimum of 100 USD to buy XRP. Assuming you don't have any crypto assets, select **USD** currency in the **You Have** field and input the value as 100. You will then be given an estimate of how much XRP you are going to receive, as in the following screenshot:

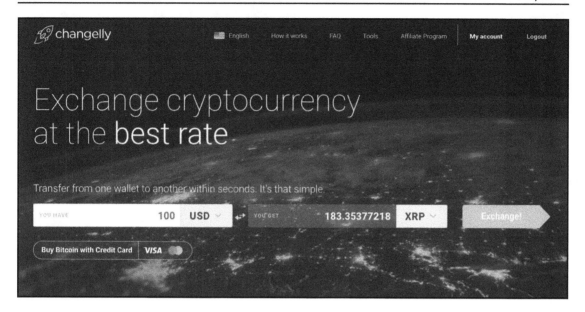

You will be taken to a confirmation screen, as shown in the following screenshot. Just confirm the details and click **Next**:

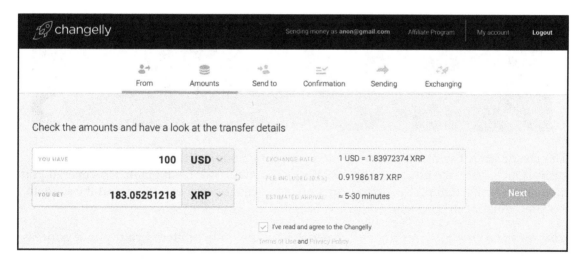

You will be asked to input your Ripple account's public address. This is the address shown below your account's nickname, highlighted in the red rectangular box in the following screenshot. Make sure you use the copy button because some parts of the address may be truncated on the display. You can paste the address here. Once changelly confirms your payment, it will automatically send the respective XRP to your public address:

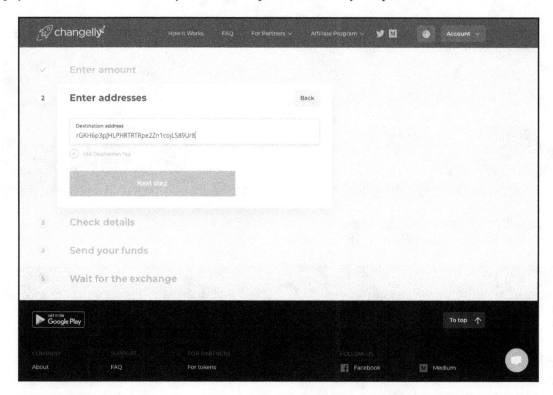

The **Destination Tag** option allows you to tag transactions so that they can be classified easily. Our Toast wallet doesn't require a destination tag, so leave it blank. However, if you are using a wallet that provides a destination tag, please ensure that you input the same in the preceding form, otherwise you won't be receiving your XRP.

You are again shown a confirmation screen. Make sure you've entered your public address accurately. Go ahead and confirm and make the payment. Once you make the payment, please wait a little while for the exchange to happen.

Here, we are sending more than 20 XRP (183 XRP) to activate the account. In this case, 20 XRP is reserved, so the account balance will be 163 XRP.

Congratulations! You've now activated your wallet.

Making an international transfer

In Ripple, there is no such thing as international transfers. Anyone can send money to anyone within seconds, irrespective of how far away they are. If you want to send money to your friend living in Israel, get their public address and destination tag (if their wallet has one).

Open Toast wallet , enter your pin, and tap on the **$** button on the bottom of the screen. You will be asked to select the account from which you want to send Ripple. You need to provide your friend's public address in the **to** field. If they have a destination tag, please add it. You can select the currency you want to send, but you need to have enough in the respective currency. You can enter the amount and tap on **pay**. You will be asked to provide your passphrase. The transfer should happen in 4-10 seconds.

In the following screenshot, I'm sending 2 Ripples to a friend:

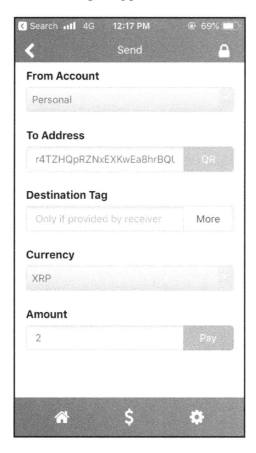

Trading XRP

In this section, we will look at how we can exchange XRP for other cryptocurrencies. You need an account in a crypto exchange to make a trade. You can use the exchange of your choice, but here we are going to use StellarX because it's a decentralized peer-peer exchange. Please go through the process of account creation in StellarX. You will also be creating a Stellar wallet in the process, so make sure you note your keys down.

Click on the **Deposit** button on the top right, as shown in following screenshot:

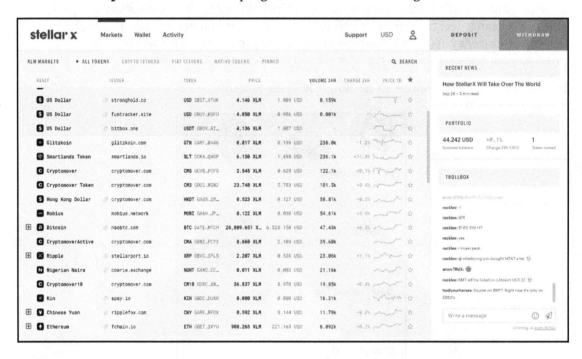

StellarX requires you to deposit more than 68 XRP.

Your XRP will be automatically converted into XLM (Stellar Lumens), as shown in the following screenshot:

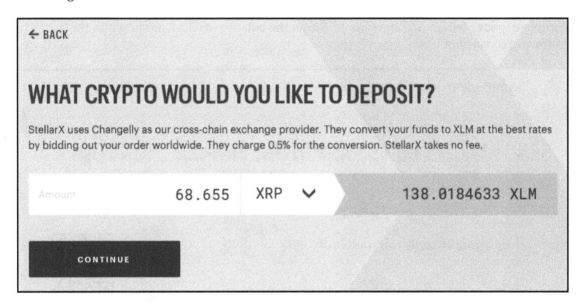

You will be asked to confirm these details in the next screen. Once you've confirmed your details, you will be asked to deposit Ripple to a specified address, as in the following screenshot. You will be provided with a destination tag. A unique destination tag helps them map the XRP deposit to your account.

You can go ahead and deposit XRP using the Toast wallet—the process is similar to sending a transaction, as we discussed earlier. However, in this case, we need to fill the destination tag field. Please allow some time for the transfer to happen. Once the transfer is complete, your StellarX account should reflect the balance in XLM, as shown in the following screenshot:

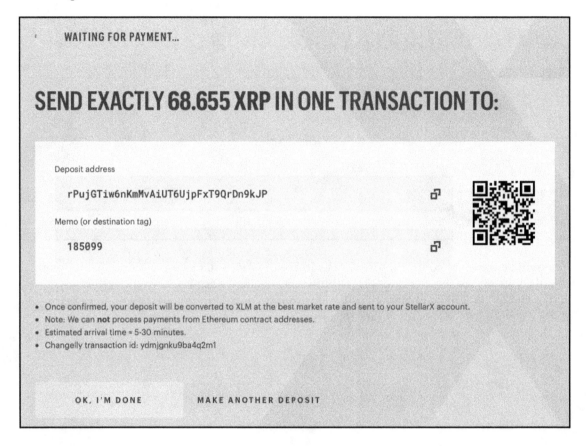

Now, let's use some of this XLM to buy Ethereum. You can enter the desired amount of ETH you want to buy. After you've entered the ETH value, click on the **Buy ETH** button, as shown in the following screenshot:

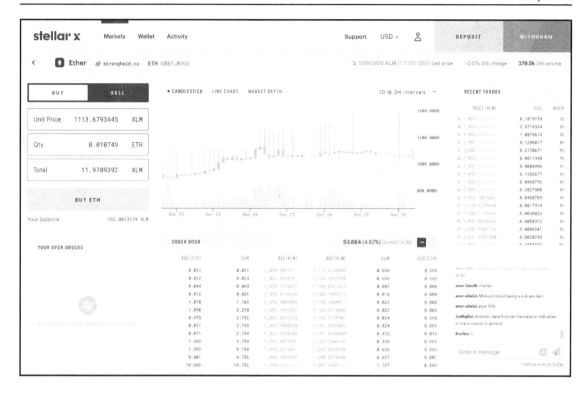

Your order should be placed almost immediately. Depending on the market, some exchanges might take some time. You should be able to see your ETH balance in the **Wallet** section once the exchange happens.

Importing an existing wallet

There are a lot of ways to generate a Ripple account. Sometimes, it is difficult for you to manage them when they aren't in one place. In this section, we will look at how you can import an existing account into Toast wallet.

To import an existing wallet, follow these steps:

1. Open Toast wallet , enter your pin, and click on the + button. You will be navigated to another screen.
2. Click on **Add Existing Address**. Now, you will be asked to provide the secret key of your Ripple account.

3. Once you have entered the secret key, set a nickname to identify your account and provide your Toast wallet's passphrase.

4. Click on **Import Account**. Your account will be immediately imported to Toast wallet.

Setting up an offline wallet

An offline wallet can help you set up a Ripple account without storing any records digitally. Since the keys are generated offline, you can be assured that the generated keys don't leave your machine. Offline wallets can provide high security because no one can hack something that doesn't exist digitally. However, they are prone to physical theft. This section is only for your reference.

 If you are happy with the desktop/mobile wallet you created earlier, you can skip this part.

Navigate to Exarpy, as shown in the following screenshot, to generate an offline wallet. It would be better to use private browsing mode, where plugins are generally disabled. This is to prevent browser plugins spying on you:

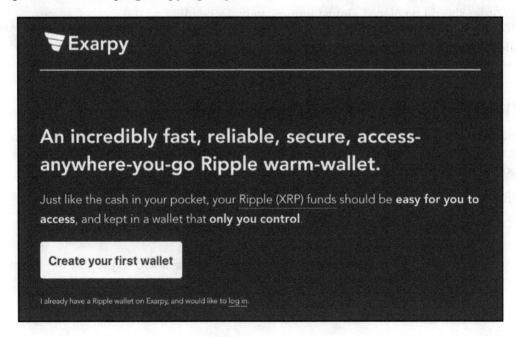

Click on **Create your first wallet**; you will be asked to go offline. If you are given additional recommendations, please follow them to make the process safer. Ensure that you disconnect yourself from the internet.

Once you are offline, you are given a brief about your PIN. Your PIN is the recovery phrase of your Ripple wallet. If you lose your secret key, you will still be able to regenerate it using your PIN. However, if you lose your recovery phrase, you will lose your funds forever. Once you agree to the terms, click on **Choose your Pin**.

You will be taken to another screen, where you will be asked to select 16 numbers, as shown in the following screenshot. Make sure you finish this process:

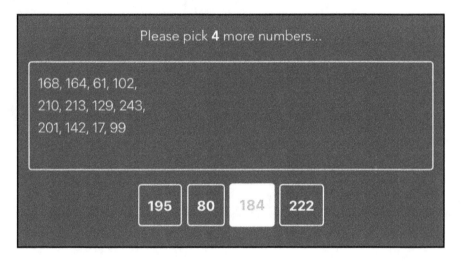

After you complete the PIN generation process, you will be shown your account credentials.

Please note that this is the first and the last time you are shown these credentials. No records are stored online or in your computer, so make sure you write them down.

The Account Verification Code and Pin are required for you to log in through Exarpy. They also provide you with a secret key. Hence, if Exarpy shuts down, you can continue using your Ripple account through other wallets by using the secret key. Once you write them down, check the radio button and click on **Great, let's log in and activate your wallet**. Please don't go online yet. The following screenshot explains the same:

Remember:

Never give your account access information anyone, as it can be used to remove all funds from your account. All transactions are **irreversible**, and **stolen funds are not recoverable**.

Please write down your **Account Verification Code**, and keep it in a safe place:

> RHL

Please write down your **PIN**, and keep it in a safe place:

> 168, 164, 61, 102,
> 210, 213, 129, 243,
> 201, 142, 17, 99,
> 222, 177, 170, 248

Please write down your **case-sensitive Secret Key**, and keep it in a safe place:

> sEd7eZpJakvzyqohHy2f3V3XUfZoeRR

○ Ok! I have my Account Verification Code, PIN, and Secret Key, written down.

You will be asked to provide your PIN and account verification code. Once you input those values, click on **Login**. Now, Exarpy will request you to go online. You would be then requested to activate your wallet. We covered this topic earlier in this chapter in the "Activating the Ripple account" section.

To see your wallet address, just click on the **skip these tutorials,...** link on the bottom of the page. You will be shown your Ripple account's dashboard. Check the radio button and agree to the terms. You will then be shown your wallet's public address, as shown in the following screenshot. You can send 20 XRP to this public address and activate your account:

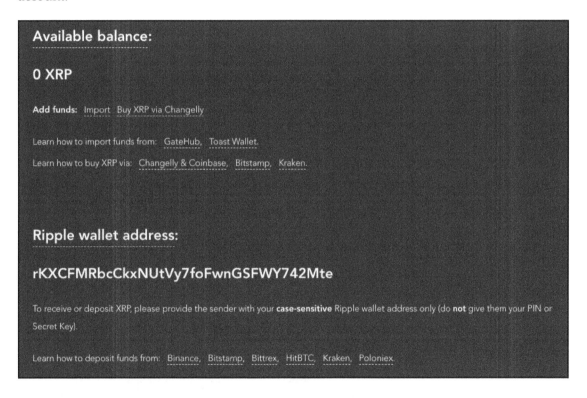

Protecting your Ripples

There have been a lot of incidents where cryptocurrencies were lost due to hacking and human error. In this section, we will look at how we can protect our Ripples.

Don't leave your Ripples on centralized exchanges

Leaving cryptocurrencies in centralized exchanges is a bad idea. Since they store these keys in a single database, when their database is compromised, our accounts can be hacked. In the past, bitcoins worth billions of dollars have been stolen from centralized exchanges. You can either use decentralized exchanges or withdraw your funds to your hardware/paper wallets. This process will be difficult for most traders, but it's a necessary precaution.

Make backups

Consider the scenarios where your computer's data gets corrupted or when your desktop/mobile/hardware wallet is lost. There is no way to recover your money. Therefore, make encrypted backups of your Ripple account on an external hard disk or in a secure place online. Here, encrypting your backup is important—do not store plain text version of your secret keys. Consider the possibility that, when your backup is stolen, your backup will still be safe if it's encrypted.

Use antivirus software

Buy and install a good antivirus software. You will be risking malware and spyware attacks otherwise. There are viruses out there that are designed to take control of your system or to spy on you. If they get hold of your secret key, your money may be lost forever. A good antivirus software will protect you from such risks.

Disable browser plugins

Though browser plugins make our life easier, they can be also used to spy on your browser's activity. It's better to use a separate browser with its plugins disabled when you make crypto transactions. Hence, you can be sure that no one is watching you while you input your secret keys.

Store Ripples in multiple wallets

You are probably aware of the saying *Don't put all your eggs in one basket*. It's safer to store your Ripples in multiple wallets. Hence, even if one of your wallets is compromised, you wouldn't risk losing all of your money.

For big sums, use cold wallets

If you want to store big sums of money, use cold wallets, since hackers cannot steal something that doesn't exist online. Make sure you protect your paper/cold wallet from physical damage and theft. If it's lost or damaged, your money is lost forever.

Use reputable wallets

There are several wallets online, so please make sure that you use reputed ones. Also, make sure that you download these wallets from their respective websites. Somebody can easily make a cloned version of these wallets and upload them online. These versions will be programmed to leak your secret keys. That would, again, result in your money being lost forever.

Important things you must remember

The following are some important points that you must remember:

- Your Ripple account won't be activated unless you send the reserve amount (presently 20 XRP) to its public address.
- Your Toast wallet 's recovery phrase won't recover your Ripple accounts unless you have a backup.
- Desktop/mobile/offline wallets give you access to Ripple account's secret key. You can use this to manage or migrate your account in their competitor's wallets.
- Some wallets provide you with a destination tag, so make sure that you provide them, along with your address, when you want to receive Ripples.
- Though offline wallets are safe from online/software attacks, they are prone to physical damage or theft.
- Don't leave your Ripples on centralized exchanges.
- When you want to store huge sums of money, use cold wallets.

Summary

In this chapter, we've learned the answers to the following questions:

- What are the types of Ripple wallets?
- How do I choose my wallet?
- How can I set up a Ripple account?
- How can I activate my Ripple account?
- How can I make an international transfer?
- How can I trade XRP?
- How can I import an existing wallet?
- How can I set up an offline wallet?
- How can I protect my Ripples?

In the next chapter, we will learn about the application of Ripple. We'll learn how Ripple can make a huge impact on banks, businesses, payment gateways, and marketplaces.

Applications of Ripple **3**

In the last chapter, we learned to work with Ripple currency. In this chapter, we'll learn the applications of Ripple. Studying the applications of Ripple will help us get insight on the future potential of Ripple. For developers, this chapter will lay a foundation for the upcoming chapters where we'll learn to code escrows and checks. We will also look into some of the common misconceptions about Ripple.

The following topics will be covered in this chapter:

- High speed and low-cost payments
- Cross-currency payments
- Checks
- Escrows
- Payment channels
- Initial coin offering
- Decentralized exchange
- Common misconceptions about Ripple

High speed and low-cost payments

In the first chapter, we learned why the global payment system was inefficient. Let's get into the following to understand how Ripple overcomes its inefficiencies:

- Present global payment systems don't work as a system. They lack effective inter-connectivity.
- Lack of effective inter-connectivity leads to costly transaction fees and delays.
- Most data in these systems is hidden and can be easily manipulated. Hence, there's no transparency in the system.
- Lack of transparency in the system increases the chances of fraud.

- High transaction costs limits banks ability to address a large market.
- Since there's no standardization across networks, it's unreliable for people to send sensitive information with their transaction.

Ripple solves the above inefficiencies through RippleNet. It uses blockchain technologies for reliable, efficient, and secure payments. Banks can integrate RippleNet into their system to make global payments efficient. Following are the reasons why RippleNet is efficient when compared with traditional payments:

- The transactions on RippleNet are atomic. They either happen or don't happen at all. There's no partial transaction success unlike in the traditional systems. This drastically eliminates failed transactions.
- Ripple uses blockchain technology to ensure fast and real-time settlements.
- Since the entities in the Ripple blockchain are effectively interconnected, it can find cost optimized payment paths to drastically reduce transaction cost.
- The transactions on a public blockchain are visible to everyone. Hence, the system is transparent.
- Sensitive information can be encrypted and sent along with transactions. Hence, users in the system can exchange messages securely.
- It brings standardization in APIs, rules, and governance. This increases the flexibility of the system. Hence, it makes it easier to build futuristic applications that meet the rising demands of consumers.

xCurrent

xCurrent is a software that sits between banks and RippleNet. It transforms traditional payment messaging formats into standard messages that're recognized by other users in RippleNet. Banks use xCurrent to make transactions that're fast, efficient, cheap and transparent. It consists of four components:

- **Messenger**: It allows banks to communicate with each other. Before making a transaction, banks can exchange with each other the KYC information, payment details, exchange rates, and so on. This allows banks to know the total cost of the transaction before even making a transaction.
- **Validator:** They confirm whether transactions are valid on a Ripple network. Multiple validators on the Ripple network reach a consensus on the state of the ledger. They work efficiently by minimizing settlement risks.

- ILP ledger: Every bank integrated with xCurrent will have the ILP ledger. It's powered by xCurrent with 24X7 availability. It automates the process of fund settlement. It will keep a track of credits, debits, liquidity, and so forth.
- **FX ticker:** If a bank wants to exchange some dollars for euros from another bank, it needs to be aware of the exchange rates. After an exchange is made, the ILP ledger needs to be updated. FX ticker is the component that facilitates such exchanges. It will provide exchange rate information between ledgers. It also enables asset exchange between ledgers and ensures transaction settlement.

How does it work?

Let's consider a simple example where company X wants to send company Y €500. However, since company X is based in the U.S., they have a U.S. bank account. Company Y has a bank account in Europe. Now, in order for the transfer to be complete, company X's bank should exchange dollars for euros and send it to company Y's bank account.

This is where xCurrent software plays an important role. Banks can provide each other with liquidity using xCurrent's ILP ledger and FX ticker components. They can set an exchange rate through and leave xCurrent to manage the heavy lifting of currency exchange and the settlement process.

Before making the transaction, banks will interact with each other through xCurrent's messenger component. They verify their customer's identity and carry out Anti Money Laundering checks. Later, company X's bank will query to find out the processing fee and the exchange cost. They find out the exchange rate of EUR/USD is at 1.5 and the processing fee would be $10. Company X also needs to bear the processing cost of their bank, which is $10.

Hence, the total amount would be $770 (*(500 * 1.5) + 10 + 10*). Company X agrees to the amount and the transaction is initiated. The sender bank takes the processing fee of $10. The amount that needs to be transferred is $760.

These funds are put on hold until the beneficiaries bank shows proof that it has put the same funds on hold to credit company Y.

Now both banks exchange cryptographic proofs that the amount is on hold. Ripple validators receive this proof and verify it. Once the validator confirms the proof, it directs the ILP ledgers of both banks to release and transfer funds. Hence, an amount of $770 would be debited from company X's account. Simultaneously, company Y's account is credited with €500. This process is atomic, either both of these transfer happens or nothing happens. Hence, the chances of settlement failure are minimized.

The following diagram describes how different components of **xCurrent** integrate with the traditional banking system to enable cross-border payments:

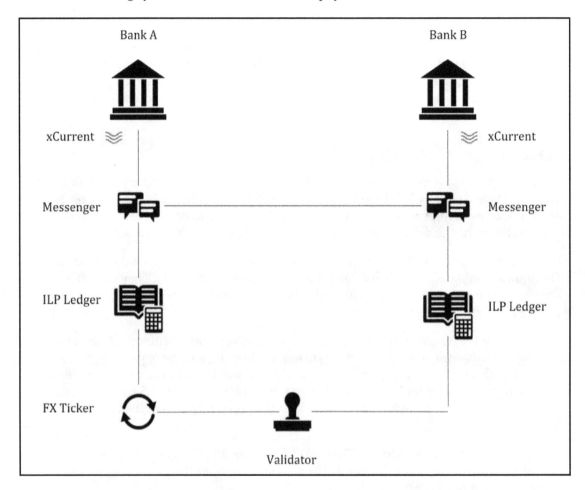

Advanced payment applications

Since Ripple uses blockchain technology, it allows applications beyond transferring money from point to point. Let's have a look at such applications.

Cross-currency payments

At the beginning of this chapter, we saw how ripple enables currency exchange through banks. However, Ripple has built-in exchange features that allow traders to create offers to exchange currencies. This enables people to send cross-currency payments through the Ripple network.

How does it work?

In the first chapter, we learned that Ripple allows you to exchange not just Ripple but anything of value. This means you can send currencies, such as USD and EUR, through Ripple. This is made possible because Ripple allows organizations or institutions to issue currency. This issued currency is tied to holdings of currency outside Ripple's ledgers. So, a bank X can issue USD in the form of an XRP ledger asset by holding the money outside.

Now, there's a problem of trust. How can you ensure that the digital asset issued you through Ripple can be redeemed for USD later? Hence, Ripple allows you to create a trust line between you and the issuer. You can select the maximum limit that an issuer can owe you. Ripple therefore uses issued currency and trust lines to enable the exchange of anything of value.

Now, let's get back to cross-currency payments. Ripple allows traders to create offers on the Ripple ledger.

Let's say John does forex trading, and he actively creates offers on Ripple's ledger book. The last offer he created was that he was willing to buy dollars for euros at a fixed exchange rate($1.25 = €1).

Paul who lives in the United States wants to send €500 to his friend in Europe. Paul comes to Ripple to make a cross-currency payment. However, there's a problem; he can't know for sure at what rates his money would be exchanged before making the transaction. He has two ways of making this cross-currency payment:

- He can send a fixed money at a variable cost to him. Here, he wants to make sure his friend receives exactly €500 and he's willing to bear the price for it.
- He can send a variable amount at a fixed cost to him. Here, he's only willing to spend $600, however, his friend might receive, say, €480, depending on the exchange rates. Such payments are called partial payments in Ripple.

Paul will be able to see the offers posted by traders on the Ripple's ledger. Since Ripple selects the offer that's the cheapest, Paul can make a guess. However, since a high volume of transaction happens in Ripple, the offer could be redeemed by someone else before Paul.

Paul decides to send a fixed money of €500 at a variable cost to him. Ripple's system checks for the best offer and finds John's offer is good. According to John's exchange rate, Paul is debited with $625. John's €500 is sent to Paul's friend and John is credited with $625. That's how Ripple makes cross-currency payments happen.

The following diagram demonstrates the flow of transaction between users through the Ripple network:

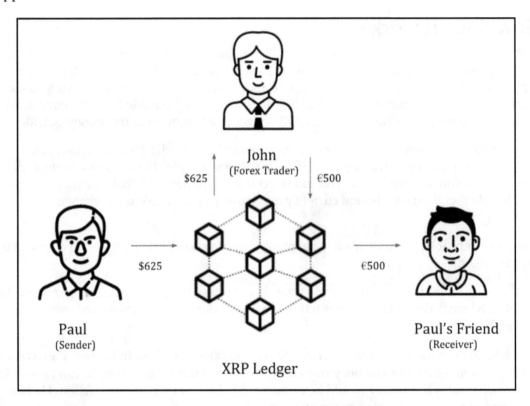

Here's an example of the `"OfferCreate"` JSON that's created by a trader who wants to buy $50:

```
{
    "TransactionType": "OfferCreate",
    "Account": "ra5nK24KXen9AHvsdFTKHSANinZseWnPcX",
    "Fee": "12",
    "Flags": 0,
    "LastLedgerSequence": 7108682,
    "Sequence": 8,
    "TakerGets": "6000000",
    "TakerPays": {
```

```
        "currency": "USD",
        "issuer": "ruazs5h1qEsqpke88pcqnaseXdm6od2xc",
        "value": "50"
    }
}
```

Checks

In order to prevent money laundering and other fraud, financial institutions are put under strict regulatory measures. They're supposed to produce documentation regarding the source of their funds. Ripple's system allows anyone to send money to any address. If this financial institution can't control the acceptance of payments, unwanted payments can become a huge burden since the institution will be obliged to pay penalties.

Ripple account holders can set deposit authorization on their accounts. This configuration will disable the account from receiving the regular payments. Now, the account will be able to receive payments only through checks, escrows, and payment channels.

We will discuss escrows and payments channels later in this chapter. Checks in Ripple work exactly like paper checks. Any user on Ripple can create a check by specifying the amount to be transferred and the receiver's address. Money is not put on hold on the sender's account while the check is created. Hence, if the sender doesn't have enough balance in their account, the recipient can't cash the check. However, like traditional checks, the recipient can try again to cash out until the check expires.

The recipient won't be able to cash out the check after it expires. The sender or the recipient is allowed to cancel the check. Hence, this allows institutions to completely control the acceptance of payments. The usage of checks isn't restricted to prevent money laundering but people can also use them to send deferred payments. Even issued currency can be sent through checks.

How does it work?

If Angel wants to send Jacob a check of 50 XRP, Angel creates a transaction JSON that specifies the amount to be transferred and Jacob's Ripple address. Later, she signs the transaction using her private key and submits it to the Ripple's network for validation by calling the `CheckCreate` function. Once the validators confirm the transaction submitted by Angel, the check would be created.

She can send this digital check to Jacob using any mode of communication. Once Jacob receives the digital check, he can cash it out by submitting it to Ripple's network by calling the `CheckCash` function. Now, validators work to confirm whether the check submitted by Jacob is authentic. Later, it checks whether Angel has enough balance for the check to be cashed out. If Angel has enough balance, she is debited 50 XRP and Jacob's account will be credited with the same amount. However, if she doesn't have enough balance, the transaction would be rejected and Jacob can attempt again until the check expires.

If Angel changes her mind, she will be able to cancel the check. In that case, when Jacob tries to cash out the check it would be rejected. Jacob also has the option to reject the payment by cancelling the check.

The following diagram demonstrates how a check is created, sent and cashed out on the Ripple network:

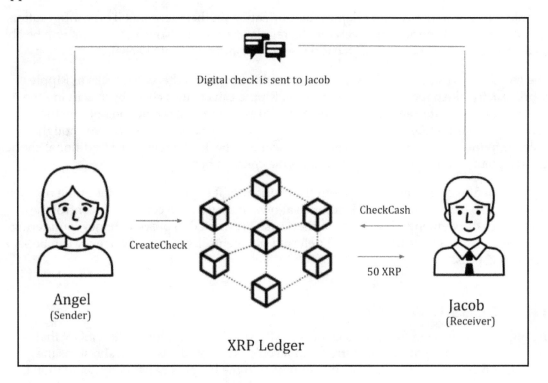

Here's an example of the `"CheckCreate"` JSON that would be used by the sender to send a check of 50 XRP:

```
{
    "TransactionType": "CheckCreate",
    "Account": "rUn84CUYbNjRoTQ6mSW7BVJPSVJNLb1QLo",
    "Destination": "rfkElaSy9G8Upk4JssnwBxhEv5p4mn2KTy",
    "SendMax": "50000000",
    "Expiration": 570113521,
    "InvoiceID":
"6F1DFD1D0FE8A32E40E1F2C05CF1C15545BAB56B617F9C6C2D63A6B704BEF59B",
    "DestinationTag": 1,
    "Fee": "12"
}
```

Here's an example of the `"CheckCash"` JSON that would be used by the receiver to redeem a sent check:

```
{
    "Account": "rfkElaSy9G8Upk4JssnwBxhEv5p4mn2KTy",
    "TransactionType": "CheckCash",
    "Amount": "50000000",
    "CheckID":
"838766BA2B995C00744175F69A1B11E32C3DBC40E64801A4056FCBD657F57334",
    "Fee": "12"
}
```

Payment channels

Payment channels are useful when a user wants to make a large volume of small payments to another user. These payments aren't immediately credited to the recipient's account. However, the recipient can claim the payments to their account at any time.

Ronat is a fitness expert and influencer on social media. Paul is the owner of a gym. He wants his gyms to gain some attention on social media. Paul approaches Ronat for help. She agrees to blog and tweet about the gym. Paul agrees to pay 30 XRP for every blog post and 10 XRP for every tweet she makes. However, he has a spending limit of 200 XRP.

Paul can start a payment channel with Ronat as the recipient. The total balance of the payment channel is set to 200 XRP. This amount will be debited from Paul's account and would be transferred to the payment channel's balance. Every time Ronat writes a blog post, Paul sends a receipt that mentions the amount he owes to Ronat. For the first post, Paul will owe Ronat 30 XRP. Later, for the second one, he will owe her 60 XRP and so on. The receipt can be sent through any mode of communication. Ronat would be able to verify these receipts. She can submit these receipts anytime on Ripple to cash out her money.

How does it work?

Paul started by creating a payment channel on Ripple by calling the "PaymentChannelCreate" function. He then specifies the total amount allocated (200 XRP), Ronat's Ripple address, and so on. This is submitted to Ripple's network for validation.

Once the payment channel is validated by the Ripple network, the payee (Ronat) can check the specifics of the payment channel. She ensures that the destination account to which the payment is sent is correct. She makes sure there's enough time set for her to cash out the receipts or claims. If her wallet has a destination tag, she also ensures that it's mentioned on the payment channel. It's important for the payee to check for the specifics of the payment channel, as any error in the specifics can result in failure of payments.

Paul now wants Ronat to blog about his gym. He creates a claim of 30 XRP and signs the claim using his private key. He sends the signed claim to Ronat using digital communication channels. Now, Ronat can verify whether the claim is valid using the "ChannelVerify" function. She ensures that the payment channel has enough balance.

Now, she can confidently provide her service. She writes a blog post about Paul's gym. This process is repeated, and Paul will continue sending claims for more blogs and tweets from Ronat.

Ronat is now done with her job. She can take the last claim from Paul, submit it to Ripple's network using the "PaymentChannelClaim" function to redeem her 200 XRP.

Now that everything ended well, Paul can request Ripple network to close the payment channel.

The following diagram demonstrates how two users can send and receive payments through payment channels:

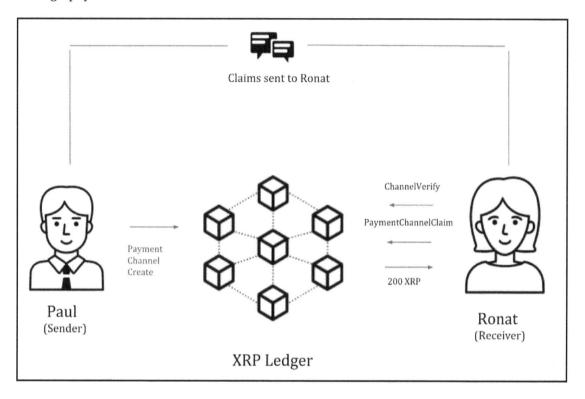

Here's an example of the `"PaymentChannelCreate"` JSON that would be used by the sender to open a payment channel with a balance of 200 XRP:

```
{
    "Account": "rf1BiGeXwwQoi8Z2ueFYTEXSwuJYfV2Jpn",
    "TransactionType": "PaymentChannelCreate",
    "Amount": "200000000",
    "Destination": "rsA2LpzuawewSBQXkiju3YQTMzW13pAAdW",
    "SettleDelay": 86400,
    "PublicKey":
"32D2471DB72B27E3310F355BB33E339BF26F8392D5A93D3BC0FC3B566612DA0F0A",
    "CancelAfter": 533171558,
    "DestinationTag": 23480,
    "SourceTag": 11747
}
```

Here's an example of the `"PaymentChannelClaim"` JSON that would be used by the receiver to claim 200 XRP to their account:

```
{
  "Channel":
"C1AE6DDDEEC05CF2978C0BAD6FE302948E9533691DC749DCDD3B9E5992CA6198",
  "Amount": "200000000",
  "Signature":
"30440220718D264EF05CAED7C781FF6DE298DCAC68D002562C9BF3A07C1E721B420C0DAB02
203A5A4779EF4D2CCC7BC3EF886676D803A9981B928D3B8ACA483B80ECA3CD7B9B",
  "PublicKey":
"32D2471DB72B27E3310F355BB33E339BF26F8392D5A93D3BC0FC3B566612DA0F0A"
}
```

Escrow

Escrow is a feature in Ripple users can use to send conditional payments. There're mainly two types of escrows, time-held and conditionally-held. Time-held escrows allow release payments after the specified time is passed. Conditionally-held escrows allow the release of payments when a cryptographic condition is fulfilled. However, Ripple's escrow doesn't support issued currencies—it only supports XRP.

Phoebe started a non-profit to help uneducated kids. She needs investment and approaches John, who's an investor. John agrees to invest 10,000 XRP. However, he doesn't want to release all the money at once. He wants to make an initial investment of 2,000 XRP, later release 4,000 XRP to Phoebe after three months, and finally release the remaining 4,000 XRP after six months. He can achieve this using time-held escrow.

John sends the initial investment of 2,000 XRP to Phoebe using Ripple's payment system. Phoebe can now use the money to start work on her project. She can hire people, rent an office, and so on.

John sets up two time-held escrows on Ripple. The first escrow is set to release funds to Phoebe's account after three months. The second escrow is set to release funds after six months. John is debited with 8,000 XRP, and these two escrows will each have 4,000 XRP locked in it.

Phoebe can be assured that she'll get funds since they are locked up in the escrow. After the first three months, Phoebe will be able to release the first escrow and redeem 4,000 XRP into her account. She'll able to release the second escrow after six months.

How does it work?

John calls the "EscrowCreate" function specifying the release time, amount, Phoebe's Ripple address and expiration time. The amount specified would be debited from John's account and will now be locked up in the newly created escrow.

Before the escrow finish/release time, no one will be able to access the locked XRP. After the release time, either John, Phoebe or any user can call the "EscrowFinish" function to release the locked up XRP into Phoebe's account.

If Phoebe doesn't redeem her money before the escrow expires, John can call the "EscrowCancel" function to return the locked up funds to his account.

The following demonstrates the working of an escrow:

1. John creates the escrow on Ripple using the "EscrowCreate" function. The amount would be 4,000 XRP and the lock period would be 3 months:

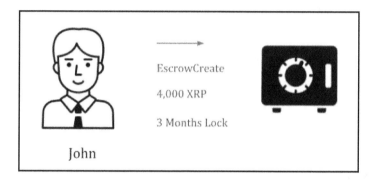

2. Phoebe calls the "EscrowFinish" function after three months:

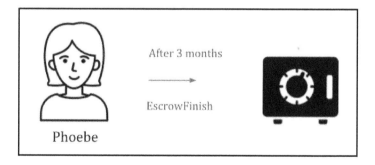

3. The Ripple network releases 4,000 XRP to Phoebe's account:

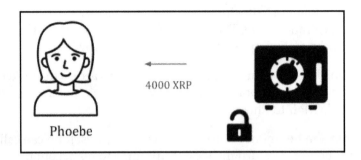

Here's an example of the `"EscrowCreate"` JSON that would be used by the creator of the XRP to lock 200 XRP:

```
{
    "Account": "rf1BiGeXwwQoi8Z2ueFYTEXSwuJYfV2Jpn",
    "TransactionType": "EscrowCreate",
    "Amount": "100000000",
    "Destination": "rsA2LpzuawewSBQXkiju3YQTMzW13pAAdW",
    "CancelAfter": 533257958,
    "FinishAfter": 533171558,
    "Condition":
"A0258020E3B0C44298FC1C149AFBF4C8996FB92427AE41E4649B934CA495991B7852B85581
0100",
    "DestinationTag": 23480,
    "SourceTag": 11747
}
```

Here's an example of the `"EscrowFinish"` JSON that can be used by anyone to send the locked funds to the destination account after the escrow finish time has lapsed:

```
{
    "Account": "rf1BiGeXwwQoi8Z2ueFYTEXSwuJYfV2Jpn",
    "TransactionType": "EscrowFinish",
    "Owner": "rf1BiGeXwwQoi8Z2ueFYTEXSwuJYfV2Jpn",
}
```

Initial coin offering

Initial coin offering is a new method to raise funds. If you have an idea, you can create a white paper and start issuing shares in your company in the form of cryptocurrencies. People who believe in your idea can buy these coins or shares. If your company becomes profitable, then the value of these coins would increase. Hence, your initial investor can sell your coins for a higher value and make profits. Some companies choose to offer utility coins, hence people who buy your coins will be able to redeem them for a service from your company at a future date.

Janet wants to start a cupcake store, but she doesn't have enough money. She requires funding of $25,000. She can use Ripple to issue JCS (Janet's Cupcake Store) coins. People who initially believe in her idea can purchase these coins. Janet can use the funding to build her cupcake store. As she starts delivering cupcakes, initial investors can use JCS coins to buy cupcakes from her store.

Decentralized exchange

Trade exchanges allow users to trade assets of value. However, most of these exchanges are centralized. Centralized exchanges hold assets of their users. If a user wants to start trading with their 1,000 XRP, they need to send this money to Ripple address of the centralized exchange to start trading. The problem with being centralized is that exchanges are highly vulnerable. In the past decade, a lot of centralized exchanges were hacked and assets worth billions of dollars were stolen.

The following is a list of past attacks and the assets stolen:

Exchange Name	Date	Asset Stolen
MtGox	March 2014	850,000 BTC
Cryptsy	July 2014	300,00 LTC & 13,000 BTC
Mintpal	December 2014	3,894 BTC
Bitstamp	January 2015	19,000 BTC
Bter	February 2015	7,000 BTC
Bitfinex	August 2016	120,00 BTC

Nicehash	December 2017	4000 BTC
Coincheck	January 2018	523,000,000 NEM
Bitgrail	February 2018	17,000,000 NANO
CoinSecure	April 2018	483 BTC

An alternative to centralized exchanges is decentralized exchanges. Decentralized exchanges enable the exchange of value without holding the user's assets. You don't have to transfer your asset to a third party for you to start trading. Here, transactions happen directly between users and no middleman is involved. Hence, decentralized exchange improves security and drastically reduces cost at the same time.

Ripple contains a functional decentralized exchange that allows users to trade issued currencies for XRP or each other. Traders who wish to buy or sell currencies can create offers on Ripple. These offers are utilized for cross-currency payments, where the sender's money is bought by the trader through their offer; later the trader's money is sent to the receiver and the currency exchange is completed. Ripple has the feature of AutoBridging to reduce exchange cost. If the direct exchange from INR to USD is costly, then Ripple automatically exchanges INR to XRP and XRP to USD to reduce exchange costs.

The following demonstrates the functionality of a decentralized exchange inside Ripple:

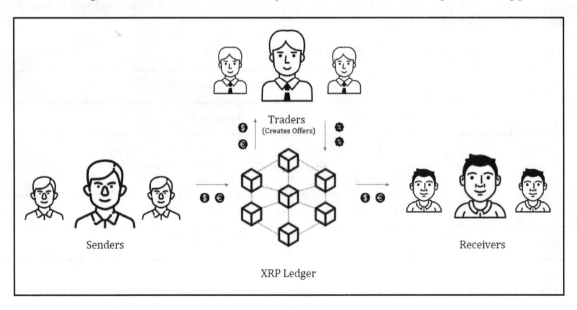

Debunking misconceptions about Ripple

Let's now look into some of the common misconceptions about Ripple. These misconceptions are important because, for investors, these lead to a make-or-break decisions.

Ripple and XRP are not the same

Ripple is a company that makes software products for banks. This company made an open-source distributed ledger or the XRP ledger. This ledger also issues its own currency called XRP. However, all of the software products that Ripple offer doesn't use this XRP ledger.

The xCurrent software we discussed in the last chapter doesn't use the XRP ledger. However, the product uses blockchain technology for cheap and fast payment settlements.

The XRP ledger is decentralized and powered by nodes around the world. However, the Ripple company is not decentralized. If the Ripple company cease to exist, the XRP ledger and its functionality won't be affected. Users would be able to use the decentralized ledger and make transactions.

This has been a misconception because, if you look at other cryptocurrencies such as Bitcoin and Ethereum, their name represents their product/ledger. However, in Ripple, the decentralized XRP ledger is one of the products of the company.

Funds lockup

Another common misconception is about the 55 billion coins that are held by Ripple. It's true that Ripple has only released a portion of XRP coins for open circulation. However, accusing them of holding the XRP coins themselves won't be totally correct.

The 55 billion coins are held in 55 escrows, with each escrow holding a billion coins. Every month, 1 billion coins are released as each of these escrows begin to expire. The released coins would be available for open circulation. The lockup was a strategic move by Ripple to ensure there are no concerns of Ripple flooding the market.

No mining

Bitcoins are circulated through a process calling mining. When people transact on Bitcoin, the unconfirmed transactions are grouped together into a block. For the block to be added to the permanent ledger, a computational puzzle should be solved. Miners compete to solve this puzzle, and the first one to solve this puzzle is rewarded with bitcoins minted out of thin air. This process is called mining.

Ripple doesn't have the process of mining. Ripple has already created 100 billion XRP. No more XRP coins would be issues. Though mining was an innovation, it adds to the computational cost. The energy requirement is high and it would take a long time for the blocks to be added to the ledger and hence the payments would be delayed.

Ripple confirms transaction using selected validators. This decreases the energy requirement and significantly reduces speed. Hence, transactions on Ripple would take only 4-6 seconds to confirm. Bitcoin transactions take around 15-25 minutes to confirm.

Limited smart contracts

Smart contracts on Ripple are limited. Ethereum provides you with a turning complete language called Solidity. This language allows you to create any kind of application. It provides complete flexibility. For example, we can make an autonomous lending and borrowing platform using solidity.

However, Ripple's escrow contracts are limited in functionality. Here, the contract is already written, and we would only be interfacing it through the APIs to create and release escrows.

There's some news about Ripple introducing a new type of smart contracts. Hopefully, they would provide us with greater flexibility.

Important things to remember

Following are some important things that we need to remember while working with Ripple:

- Ripple solves the previous inefficiencies through RippleNet. It uses blockchain technologies for reliable, efficient, and secure payments. Banks can integrate RippleNet into their system to make global payments efficient.
- xCurrent is a software that sits between banks and RippleNet. It transforms traditional payment messaging formats into standard messages that are recognized by other users in RippleNet.
- Ripple has built-in exchange features that allow traders to create offers to exchange currencies. This enables people to send cross-currency payments through the Ripple network.
- Ripple account holders can set deposit authorization on their accounts. This configuration will disable the account from receiving the regular payments. Now, the account will be able to receive payments only through checks, escrows, and payment channels.
- Money isn't put on hold on the sender's account while the check is created. Hence, if the sender doesn't have enough balance in their account, the recipient can't cash the check. However, like traditional checks, the recipient can try again to cash out until the check expires.
- Payment channels are useful when a user wants to make a large volume of small payments to another user. These payments aren't immediately credited to the recipient's account. However, the recipient can claim the payments to their account at any time.
- Escrow is a feature in Ripple that users can use to send conditional payments. There're mainly two types of escrows, time-held and conditionally-held. Time-held escrows allow release payments after the specified time is passed. Conditionally-held escrows allow the release of payments when a cryptographic condition is fulfilled. However, Ripple's escrow doesn't support issued currencies; it only supports XRP.
- Ripple contains a functional decentralized exchange that allows users to trade issued currencies for XRP or each other.

Summary

In this chapter, we have learned answers to the following questions :

- How has Ripple solve inefficiencies of traditional systems to make payments fast and cheap?
- What are the applications of Ripple?
- What are cross-currency payments?
- How do cross-currency payments work?
- What are checks in Ripple?
- How do checks work in Ripple?
- What's an escrow in Ripple?
- How does an escrow work in Ripple?
- What are payment channels in Ripple?
- How does a payment channel in Ripple work?
- What is an ICO?
- What is a decentralized exchange?
- What's the difference between Ripple, XRP, and the XRP ledger?
- Has Ripple kept a large amount of XRP from open circulation?
- Why is Ripple faster when compared to Bitcoin?
- What are the limitations of Ripple's smart contracts?

In the next chapter, we'll learn how to connect to the Ripple network and send money using the Ripple API.

Getting Started with the Ripple API

4

In the previous chapter, we learned the applications of Ripple in theory. If you've never worked on a blockchain-based system, this chapter would be a good place to start. In this chapter, we'll take a hands-on approach and learn to work with Ripple's blockchain. If you are a developer who is familiar with APIs, this should be a piece of cake. This chapter will lay the foundation to the upcoming chapter where you'll learn to work with the check and escrow features of Ripple. The important thing you must understand is Ripple helps you program the flow of money. Earlier, money used to move slowly because of the manual work involved. Ripple provides you with a system that drastically increases the velocity of money. This opens us to a new world of possibilities. A decentralized payment blockchain is waiting to answer your call, so let's get started.

In this chapter, we'll cover the following topics:

- Connecting to the Ripple test network
- Setting up the development environment
- Fetching details of a Ripple account
- Sending money to a Ripple account
- Using the Ripple API to build web applications

Connecting to the Ripple test network

Ripple provides you with a test network to help you to test the application without using real funds. Let's go ahead and create a test net account and load it with enough XRP. This XRP doesn't have any value, and it can be only used for testing purposes. In order to create a test net account, navigate to `https://developers.ripple.com/xrp-test-net-faucet.html`.

You'll see a screen similar to the one shown in the following screenshot:

Home > Dev Tools > XRP Test Net Faucet

Test Net Servers

XRP Test Net Faucet

Use the following addresses to connect to the XRP Test Net and send transactions from your account.

Ripple has created this alternative XRP Ledger test network with nodes in every region of the world to provide a testing platform for any software products built on the XRP Ledger without using real funds.

Websockets and Ripple API

wss://s.altnet.rippletest.net:51233

Test Net funds are intended for **testing** only. The Test Net ledger and balances will be reset on a regular basis.

JSON-RPC

https://s.altnet.rippletest.net:51234

Generate credentials

Your Credentials

Address

rDMoMsL542NiEUexAAdKB4DLNLTtd6PWFp

Secret

snk1LvUcrpnqZzrYzNJV2gxUqfpXJ

Balance

10,000 XRP

Click on **Generate credentials**, and your Ripple address and secret will be generated. Your account will also be loaded with a balance of 10,000 XRP. The addresses on the right side of the screenshot are the ones we'll be using to interface with the test network. Make sure you save the Ripple address and the secret; we'll be using it to develop applications.

You can get all of the code in this chapter from this GitHub repository: `https://github.com/PacktPublishing/Ripple-Quick-Start-Guide`.

Setting up the development environment

You need to have NodeJS and npm installed in your system (node version 4.x or higher).

Let's start by creating a directory. The command is the one given in the following:

```
mkdir MyFirstRippleApp && cd MyFirstRippleApp
```

Now, let's create `package.json` in our newly created directory as shown in the following, which will install the dependencies we need to work with Ripple's APIs:

```
{
  "name": "my_ripple_experiment",
  "version": "0.0.1",
  "license": "MIT",
  "private": true,
  "//": "Change the license to something appropriate. You may want to use
'UNLICENSED' if you are just starting out.",
  "dependencies": {
    "ripple-lib": "*",
    "babel-cli": "^6.0.0",
    "babel-preset-es2015": "*"
  },
  "babel": {
    "presets": ["es2015"]
  },
  "devDependencies": {
    "eslint": "*"
  }
}
```

Let's run the following command to install the required packages:

```
npm install
```

Great, we have everything set up, so let's make our first application.

First Ripple application

In our first application, we'll write a simple program to connect to the network and fetch the account details of a specific Ripple address.

Here's the code that connects to the Ripple test network and fetches the account details of the address: `'r41sFTd4rftxY1VCn5ZDDipb4KaV5VLFy2'`. Let's run this code first and then get into the details to learn how it works. Save the following code into a file and give it the name `'get_account.js'`:

```
'use strict';
const RippleAPI = require('ripple-lib').RippleAPI;

const api = new RippleAPI({
  server: 'wss://s.altnet.rippletest.net:51233' // Ripple Test Network
  Address
```

```
});

api.connect().then(() => {
 const accountAddress = 'r41sFTd4rftxY1VCn5ZDDipb4KaV5VLFy2';

 console.log('Fetching account details of', accountAddress);
 return api.getAccountInfo(accountAddress);

}).then(info => {
 console.log(info);
 console.log('Account Details Fetched');
}).then(() => {
 return api.disconnect();
}).then(() => {
 console.log('Disconnected from the testnet.');
}).catch(console.error);
```

In order to execute the code, use the following command:

./node_modules/.bin/babel-node get_account.js

You'll see the following output. As you can see, the XRP balance says 10,000:

```
Febins-MacBook-Air:MyFirstRippleApp febinjohnjames$ ./node_modules/.bin/babel-node get_account.js
Fetching account details of r41sFTd4rftxY1VCn5ZDDipb4KaV5VLFy2
{ sequence: 1,
  xrpBalance: '10000',
  ownerCount: 0,
  previousAffectingTransactionID: '0A74D42F89CD2130E6B30CDA1A6ADA8118457491AD19AB036C3BB16E3FA204DF',
  previousAffectingTransactionLedgerVersion: 15203429 }
Account Details Fetched
Disconnected from the test net.
```

Now, let's understand how the code works.

First, we import the Ripple library, so that we can use its functions. For importing the library, we use this command:

```
const RippleAPI = require('ripple-lib').RippleAPI;
```

Then, we define which network we want to connect to. We are connecting to the test network in the following line of code; you can connect to the main network or even a local server. If you want to connect to the main network, it's recommended you run your own rippled server since the public servers are not meant for business use. You can get more information about this in the Ripple Developer Docs. The following line of code connects us to the test network:

```
const api = new RippleAPI({
  server: 'wss://s.altnet.rippletest.net:51233' // Ripple Test Network
Address
});
```

Once we have defined which network we want to connect to, we'll make the connection by calling the connect function. Once the connection is made, we'll define the Ripple address for which the account details must be fetched. We're also making the calling to fetch account details using the function getAccountInfo as seen in the following code:

```
api.connect().then(() => {
  const accountAddress = 'r41sFTd4rftxY1VCn5ZDDipb4KaV5VLFy2';

  console.log('Fetching account details of', accountAddress);
  return api.getAccountInfo(accountAddress);

})
```

If the function call is successfully done, then we'll log the output from the function using the following code:

```
.then(info => {
  console.log(info);
  console.log('Account Details Fetched');
})
```

Since we've opened a WebSocket connection, we need to disconnect. If anything goes wrong during the entire process, we also need to catch the error. The following code takes care of these things:

```
.then(() => {
  return api.disconnect();
}).then(() => {
  console.log('Disconnected from the testnet.');
}).catch(console.error);
```

Now, let's use the following code to build a simple web app. Let's get this code running and then we'll get into the details of how it works. Some browsers allow execution of this code without giving issues. If your browser is throwing permission errors, please install the XAMP or WAMP server and place these files in the `htdocs` folder. Then, navigate to the respective URL:

```html
<!DOCTYPE html>
<html>
<title> Get Account </title>
<head>
  <link rel="stylesheet" href="css/bootstrap.min.css">
</head>
<body>

<nav class="navbar navbar-expand-lg navbar-dark bg-dark">
  <a class="navbar-brand" href="#">Get Account</a>
</nav>

<br/><br/><br/>

<center>
  <p class="lead">Ripple Address : r41sFTd4rftxY1VCn5ZDDipb4KaV5VLFy2 </p>
  <p id="balance"> Please wait, fetching account details...</p>
</center>

</body>

<script src="js/lodash.js"></script>
<script src="js/jquery.min.js"></script>
<script src="js/ripple.min.js"></script>

  <script>
    var api = new
ripple.RippleAPI({server:'wss://s.altnet.rippletest.net:51233'});

    $('document').ready(function(){
      updateAccountDetails();
    });

    function updateAccountDetails(){

      api.connect().then(() => {
        const accountAddress = 'r41sFTd4rftxY1VCn5ZDDipb4KaV5VLFy2';
        return api.getAccountInfo(accountAddress);
      }).then(info => {
        $('#balance').text("Account Balance : " + info.xrpBalance+ " XRP");
      }).then(() => {
```

```
        return api.disconnect();
      }).catch(console.error);
  }

  </script>
</html>
```

Save this file as `get_account.html`. You also need to create two folders named `js` and `css` and place them in the same directory.

You will need the following `javascript` and `css` libraries for the app to work. You can download them from the following links:

- `https://cdnjs.cloudflare.com/ajax/libs/lodash.js/4.15.0/lodash.js`
- `https://code.jquery.com/jquery-3.3.1.min.js`
- `https://github.com/ripple/ripple-lib/releases/download/1.1.2/ripple-1.1.2-min.js`
- `https://maxcdn.bootstrapcdn.com/bootstrap/4.0.0/css/bootstrap.min.css`
- `https://stackpath.bootstrapcdn.com/bootstrap/4.1.3/js/bootstrap.min.js`

Download these files and save them in the `js` and `css` folders. Make sure you rename the filenames to `jquery.min.js` and `ripple.min.js`.

Alternatively, you can use the files in this book's GitHub repository. Now, you can open `get_account.html` on your browser. If everything goes well, you should be able to see the following screen:

Get Account

Ripple Address : r41sFTd4rftxY1VCn5ZDDipb4KaV5VLFy2

Account Balance : 10000 XRP

Let's now try to understand the code.

We need the `lodash` and Ripple library to interface with the Ripple network as shown in the following. We'll be using `jquery` to manipulate the DOM elements:

```
<script src="js/lodash.js"></script>
<script src="js/jquery.min.js"></script>
<script src="js/bootstrap.min.js"></script>
<script src="js/ripple.min.js"></script>
```

First, we wait for the document to get ready. Then, we connect to Ripple's test network and fetch the account details. The following lines of code parse and update the frontend using `jquery` as it receives data from Ripple:

```
var api = new
ripple.RippleAPI({server:'wss://s.altnet.rippletest.net:51233'});

    $('document').ready(function(){
      updateAccountDetails();
    });

    function updateAccountDetails(){

      api.connect().then(() => {
        const accountAddress = 'r41sFTd4rftxY1VCn5ZDDipb4KaV5VLFy2';
        return api.getAccountInfo(accountAddress);
      }).then(info => {
        $('#balance').text("Account Balance : " + info.xrpBalance+ " XRP");
      }).then(() => {
        return api.disconnect();
      }).catch(console.error);
    }

    </script>
```

In the previous code, we hard-coded the Ripple address. Let's make it dynamic so that users can input the address and fetch balance of any Ripple account. To achieve this we need to make a few modifications.

First, we need a form to input the Ripple address. Here's the code for the input form. When the user clicks on the fetch balance button, the update account details function mentioned in the previous block is triggered:

```
<form style="width:50%">
<div class="form-group">
<label for="inputRippleAddress">Ripple Address</label>
<input type="text" class="form-control" id="inputRippleAddress" aria-
describedby="rippleAddressHelp" placeholder="Enter Ripple Address">
</div>
```

```
<button onclick="updateAccountDetails()" class="btn btn-primary">Fetch
Balance</button>
</form>
```

Later, we disable the default form submit using the following lines of code:

```
$("form").submit(function(e) {
    e.preventDefault();
});
```

In the update account details function, we'll add the following line to fetch the address from the input form:

```
const accountAddress = $("#inputRippleAddress").val();
```

If you need help, you can refer to the source code in our GitHub repository.

After making these modifications, you can run it on a browser. If everything goes well, you should be able to see the screen similar to this one:

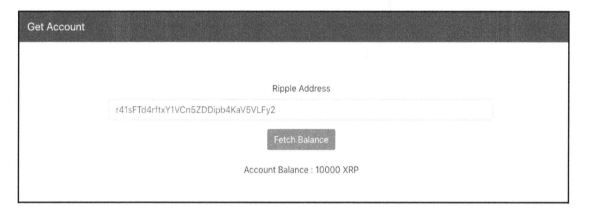

Now any user can use this app to fetch the balance of any account on Ripple.

 Remember, we're still on the test network. If you want to fetch the account balance of addresses on the main network, you need to change the server URL.

Congratulations, you have completed making your first app using Ripple's APIs.

Sending money

Now, let's learn how to send money from a Ripple account. In order to send money, we need to accomplish three things:

- **Prepare transaction**: Here we define the source address, destination address, amount to be paid, and so on.

- **Sign transaction:** You need to sign the transaction cryptographically with your secret key. This proves that you own this account.

- **Submit transaction:** Once you sign the transaction, you need to submit it to the Ripple network for validation. Your transaction would be only applied to the ledger when the validators approve your transaction.

Prepare transaction

We prepare the transaction by defining the structure as per the specification mentioned in Ripple API's documentation. We define the source address, destination address, amount, currency type, and so on. The "preparePayment" function that follows inputs the data to prepare a standard JSON that can be signed and submitted to the network:

```
'use strict';
const RippleAPI = require('ripple-lib').RippleAPI;
const api = new RippleAPI({
server: 'wss://s.altnet.rippletest.net:51233' // Ripple Test Network
Address
});

const instructions = {};
const sourceAddress = 'r41sFTd4rftxY1VCn5ZDDipb4KaV5VLFy2';
const sourceSecret = 'sptkAoSPzHq8mKLWrjU33EDj7v96u';
const destinationAddress = 'rMLhQ61cGQ3kcsGMFugYJV9QjP31BiMXav'

const amount = '50';
const instructions = {};

const transaction = {
source: {
address: sourceAddress,
maxAmount: {
value: amount,
currency: 'XRP'
```

```
}},
destination: {
address: destinationAddress,
amount: {
value: amount,
currency: 'XRP'
}}};

api.preparePayment(sourceAddress, transaction, instructions);
```

Sign transaction

We need to sign the transaction using our secret key to prove that we own the Ripple account and we are authorized to send money. The `api.sign` function mentioned in the following takes the prepared JSON from the previous step and our account's secret key as input to sign the transaction. Your secret key is used to sign the transaction locally and it isn't sent to the Ripple network:

```
const {signedTransaction} = api.sign(prepared.txJSON, sourceSecret);
```

Submit transaction

Even though we've signed the transaction, until the signed message reaches the network, no changes will occur. Once we submit the transaction, we need to wait for the validators to confirm it. When the validators approve the transaction, ledger values will change and account balances will be updated. The following function takes signed transaction as input and submits it to the network:

```
api.submit(signedTransaction).then(onSuccess,onFailure);
```

In the following lines, we've put together the code to prepare, sign, and submit the transaction. As you can see, we wait for each step to return a response before we continue to the next step:

```
api.connect().then(() => {

console.log('Connected to the test network.');
return api.preparePayment(sourceAddress, transaction,
instructions).then(prepared => {
console.log('Payment transaction is now prepared.');
const {signedTransaction} = api.sign(prepared.txJSON, sourceSecret);
console.log('Payment transaction is now signed.');
api.submit(signedTransaction).then(onSuccess,onFailure);
```

```
});
});
```

In the previous block, we added a callback to the submit transaction function. We have to be prepared to handle both success and failure. In the following lines, we handle the success and failure callbacks:

```
function onSuccess(message){
console.log("Transaction Successfully Submitted.");
console.log(message);
disconnect();
}

function onFailure(message){
console.log("Transaction Submission Failed.");
console.log(message);
disconnect();
}

function disconnect(){
api.disconnect().then(()=> {
console.log("Disconnected from test network.")
})
}
```

The previous blocks of code send 50 XRP from one Ripple account to another. Save them to the file `send_money.js`. If you need help. please refer to the `source code in our GitHub repository`.

Let's run the previous code using this command:

```
./node_modules/.bin/babel-node send_money.js
```

If everything goes well, you should see output similar to the following:

```
[Febins-MacBook-Air:SendMoney febinjohnjames$ ./node_modules/.bin/babel-node send_money.js
Connected to the test network.
Payment transaction is now prepared.
Payment transaction is now signed.
Transaction Successfully Submitted.
{ resultCode: 'tesSUCCESS',
  resultMessage: 'The transaction was applied. Only final in a validated ledger.',
  engine_result: 'tesSUCCESS',
  engine_result_code: 0,
  engine_result_message: 'The transaction was applied. Only final in a validated ledger.',
  tx_blob: '12000002280000000240000000E201B00E852A4614000000002FAF0806840000000000000000C73210247A93474AFDBA3962177E92624843403C99A8E8B46B56430FF
B4AEA9212DB6927446304402206085486D536797A96376EB429110BF57D56A714DCB0656C4A9DA2D8FEAEF8C87022044654C8D27A1B07E8C15755714177EF6176DADAC3928E70B
26AA247F408D95FF8114EFD1CAC7F8FC974342DED53BD4B1ABEDDEFD3A5E8314DEFD43AF17877C71BF8B4B0E5938D1A700AEA952',
  tx_json:
   { Account: 'r41sFTd4rftxY1VCn5ZDDipb4KaV5VLFy2',
     Amount: '50000000',
     Destination: 'rMLhQ61cGQ3kcsGMFugYJV9QjP31BiMXav',
     Fee: '12',
     Flags: 2147483648,
     LastLedgerSequence: 15225508,
     Sequence: 14,
     SigningPubKey: '0247A93474AFDBA3962177E92624843403C99A8E8B46B56430FFB4AEA9212DB692',
     TransactionType: 'Payment',
     TxnSignature: '304402206085486D536797A96376EB429110BF57D56A714DCB0656C4A9DA2D8FEAEF8C87022044654C8D27A1B07E8C15755714177EF6176DADAC3928E7
0B26AA247F408D95FF',
     hash: 'BE5759E268265E36BA5C2804267F882AA9A001D3A0AC17F75EE2B1AA6148E26A' } }
Disconnected from test network.
```

Let's check the account balance of the destination address using our previous app to make sure our money was successfully sent.

If your transaction was successful, the account balance of the destination should get updated as shown in the following screenshot:

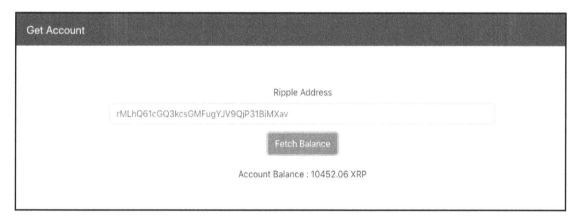

Now, let's use this code to build a web application that provides us with a graphical interface to log in and sends money.

Let's make a login modal that takes a Ripple address and secret as input and stores it in the local storage. We will be using it later to sign and submit transactions. The HTML code for the login modal is given in the following:

```
<div class="modal fade" id="loginModal" tabindex="-1" role="dialog" aria-
labelledby="loginModalLabel" aria-hidden="true">
<div class="modal-dialog" role="document">
<div class="modal-content">
<div class="modal-header">
<h5 class="modal-title" id="loginModalLabel">Login</h5>
<button type="button" class="close" data-dismiss="modal" aria-
label="Close">
<span aria-hidden="true">&times;</span>
</button>
</div>
<div class="modal-body">
<form>
<div class="form-group">
<label for="inputRippleAddress">Ripple Address</label>
<input type="text" class="form-control" id="inputRippleAddress" aria-
describedby="rippleAddressHelp" placeholder="Enter Ripple Address">
</div>
<div class="form-group">
<label for="inputSecret">Secret</label>
<input type="password" class="form-control" id="inputSecret"
placeholder="Secret">
</div>
<button onclick="storeCredentials()" class="btn btn-primary">Login</button>
</form>
</div>
</div>
</div>
</div>
```

When the user clicks on the login button, we are calling the `"storeCredentials"` function to store the address and secret. We won't be verifying whether the secret key is valid, but it'll throw an error when you try to sign the transaction.

Here's the function to store credentials:

```
function storeCredentials(){
localStorage.setItem("rippleAddress", $('#inputRippleAddress').val());
localStorage.setItem("secret", $('#inputSecret').val());
localStorage.setItem("loggedIn", true);
$('#loginModal').modal('hide');
updateAccount();
}
```

Once the credentials are stored, we need to update the UI to reflect the Ripple address and its balance.

 Storing the credentials as raw text is a bad idea. It's a good security practice to encrypt it. But, for the purpose of this tutorial, we'll ignore this step.

Use the following code to update the UI:

```
function updateAccount(){
$('#rippleAddress').text(localStorage.getItem('rippleAddress'));
updateBalance();
}

function updateBalance(){
api.connect().then(() => {
const accountAddress = localStorage.getItem("rippleAddress");
return api.getAccountInfo(accountAddress);
}).then(info => {
$('#balance').text("Account Balance : " + info.xrpBalance+ " XRP");
}).then(() => {
return api.disconnect();
}).catch(console.error);
}
```

The update account function fetches the address from the local storage and injects it into the HTML. The update balance function used the same code as in our previous app to fetch the account balance.

Now, let's build an interface that would help the user send money. In order to do that, let's create another modal by using the following code:

```
<div class="modal fade" id="sendMoneyModal" tabindex="-1" role="dialog"
aria-labelledby="sendMoneyModalLabel" aria-hidden="true">
<div class="modal-dialog" role="document">
<div class="modal-content">
<div class="modal-header">
<h5 class="modal-title" id="sendMoneyModalLabel">Send Money </h5>
<button type="button" class="close" data-dismiss="modal" aria-
label="Close">
<span aria-hidden="true">&times;</span>
</button>
</div>
<div class="modal-body">
<form>
<div class="form-group">
```

```
<label for="inputDestinationRippleAddress">Ripple Address</label>
<input type="text" class="form-control" id="inputDestinationRippleAddress"
aria-describedby="destinationRippleAddressHelp" placeholder="Destination
Ripple Address">
</div>
<div class="form-group">
<label for="inputAmount">Amount</label>
<input type="number" class="form-control" id="inputAmount"
placeholder="Amount">
</div>
<button onclick="sendMoney()" class="btn btn-primary">Send</button>
<br/> <br/>
<div class="progress">
<div class="progress-bar progress-bar-striped bg-info" role="progressbar"
style="width: 0%" aria-valuenow="0" aria-valuemin="0" aria-
valuemax="100"></div>
</div>
</form>
</div>
</div>
</div>
</div>
```

The previous form takes the destination Ripple address to which you want to send money and the amount as input. It calls the send money function. Let's have a look at the send money function that's given in the following:

```
function sendMoney(){
$('.progress').show();
const instructions = {};
const sourceAddress = localStorage.getItem('rippleAddress');
const sourceSecret = localStorage.getItem('secret');
const destinationAddress = $('#inputDestinationRippleAddress').val();
const transaction = {
source: {
address: sourceAddress,
maxAmount: {
value: $('#inputAmount').val(),
currency: 'XRP'
}
},
destination: {
address: destinationAddress,
amount: {
value: $('#inputAmount').val(),
currency: 'XRP'
}
}
```

```
};
api.connect().then(() => {
return api.preparePayment(sourceAddress, transaction,
instructions).then(prepared => {
$('.progress-bar').css('width', 40+'%').attr('aria-valuenow', 40);
const {signedTransaction} = api.sign(prepared.txJSON, sourceSecret);
api.submit(signedTransaction).then(onSuccess,onFailure);
});
});
}
```

It's almost similar to the code we used before to send money. Except here, we're fetching the Ripple address and secret from the local storage. We're also fetching the destination Ripple address from the send money form. We've added a progress bar to provide a better user experience. Once the submit transaction returns, we call the on success function to update the account balance and show an alert to the user that the transaction was submitted successfully. In the case of failure, we alert them of the same.

Here's the code for that:

```
function onSuccess(message){
$('.progress-bar').css('width', 100+'%').attr('aria-valuenow', 100);
$('#balance').text("Fetching updated balance, please wait.");
setTimeout(updateBalance, 6000);
bootstrap_alert.success('Transaction Submitted Successfully');
clear();
}

function onFailure(message){
$('.progress-bar').css('width', 100+'%').attr('aria-valuenow', 100);
bootstrap_alert.danger('Transaction Submission Failed');
clear();
}
```

If the user has already logged in, then we need code to fetch the Ripple address and update in on the display; here's the code for doing that:

```
function login(){
    if(!localStorage.getItem("loggedIn")){
      $('#loginModal').modal('show');
    } else{
      updateAccount();
    }
  }
```

We also need the logout functionality. Here's the code that helps us achieve that:

```
function logout(){ localStorage.clear(); clearInterval(fetchBalance);
location.reload(); }
```

That's almost all of the code we need. There's some basic HTML and JavaScript code to get this app running that's not mentioned in this chapter. They're elementary stuff such as showing the login/send money modal. If you need help, please refer to the `source code in our GitHub repository`.

You can save the previous blocks of code into the `send_money.html` file. If everything works fine, you should be able to see the login screen as follows:

Once you log in, you should be able to see your balance and a button to send money:

Now, let's try sending some money:

If everything goes well, you should be able to see the **Transaction Submitted Successfully** message. You should be able to see the updated account balance in 6-8 seconds. You can use the previous app to check whether the destination account is credited with the respective amount of XRP.

Congratulations, you've made an app that allows users to transact on the Ripple network.

Summary

In this chapter, we learned the answers to the following questions:

- How can we connect to the Ripple test network?
- How can we set up the development environment?
- How can we check the balance of an account using the Ripple API?
- How can we send money into a Ripple account?

In the next chapter, we'll learn how to build applications using the check and escrow features of Ripple.

5
Developing Applications Using the Ripple API

In the previous chapter, we learned to use the Ripple API to send money into a Ripple account. In this chapter, we'll learn to use the check and Escrow features of Ripple to make banking applications.

In this chapter, we'll cover the following topics:

- Sending checks
- Cashing checks
- Creating and releasing a time-held escrow
- Creating and releasing a conditionally-held escrow

Sending checks

Now, let's learn how to send checks from a Ripple account. In order to send checks, we need to accomplish the following three things. The process is similar to sending money:

1. **Prepare transaction**: Here we define the destination address, amount to be paid, and so on.
2. **Sign transaction:** You need to sign the transaction cryptographically with your secret key. This proves that you own this account.
3. **Submit transaction:** Once you sign the transaction, you need to submit it to the Ripple network for validation. Your check would become valid only when the validators approve your transaction.

In order to create a check, we would be using the "CheckCreate" method. The following code takes the destination and amount to be paid as input and generates the transaction JSON as output. You need to own the recipient account since we would be using it to cash out the check later. You need to create another Ripple account from the Ripple test net faucet as we did earlier:

```
api.prepareCheckCreate(sender, {
    "destination": receiver,
    "sendMax": {
        "currency": "XRP",
        "value": "100"
    }
}, options);
```

We would be using the following code to sign and submit the transaction to the network. It's the same methods we used to send money:

```
const {signedTransaction} = api.sign(prepared.txJSON, secret);
api.submit(signedTransaction).then(onSuccess,onFailure);
```

Once we submit the transaction to the network, we need to calculate the check ID. You need to communicate the check ID to the recipient so that they can use it to cash out the check. Here's the code to calculate check ID:

```
const checkIDhasher = createHash('sha512')
checkIDhasher.update(Buffer.from('0043', 'hex'))
checkIDhasher.update(new Buffer(decodeAddress(sender)))
const seqBuf = Buffer.alloc(4)
seqBuf.writeUInt32BE(message['tx_json']['Sequence'], 0)
checkIDhasher.update(seqBuf)
const checkID = checkIDhasher.digest('hex').slice(0,64).toUpperCase()
```

Let's put everything together:

```
'use strict';
const RippleAPI = require('ripple-lib').RippleAPI;
const decodeAddress = require('ripple-address-codec').decodeAddress;
const createHash = require('crypto').createHash;

const sender = 'r41sFTd4rftxY1VCn5ZDDipb4KaV5VLFy2';
const receiver = 'r42Qv8NwggeMWnpKcxMkx7qTtB23GYLHBX';
const secret = 'sptkAoSPzHq8mKLWrjU33EDj7v96u';
const options = {};

const api = new RippleAPI({server: 'wss://s.altnet.rippletest.net:51233'});
api.connect().then(() => {
  console.log('Connected to the test network.');
```

```
    return api.prepareCheckCreate(sender, {
      "destination": receiver,
      "sendMax": {
        "currency": "XRP",
        "value": "100"
      }
    }, options);

}).then(prepared => {
  console.log("Transaction JSON:", prepared.txJSON);
  const {signedTransaction} = api.sign(prepared.txJSON, secret);
  console.log("Transaction Signed.")
  api.submit(signedTransaction).then(onSuccess,onFailure);
});

function onSuccess(message){
  console.log(message);
  console.log("Transaction Successfully Submitted.");
  const checkIDhasher = createHash('sha512');
  checkIDhasher.update(Buffer.from('0043', 'hex'));
  checkIDhasher.update(new Buffer(decodeAddress(sender)));
  const seqBuf = Buffer.alloc(4);
  seqBuf.writeUInt32BE(message['tx_json']['Sequence'], 0);
  checkIDhasher.update(seqBuf);
  const checkID = checkIDhasher.digest('hex').slice(0,64).toUpperCase();
  console.log("CheckID:", checkID);
  disconnect();
}

function onFailure(message){
  console.log("Transaction Submission Failed.");
  console.log(message);
  disconnect();
}

function disconnect(){
  api.disconnect().then(()=> {
    console.log("Disconnected from test network.")
  });
}
```

Save this as `send_check.js`. Let's execute the code by running the following command:

```
./node_modules/.bin/babel-node send_check.js
```

If everything goes fine, you'll get the following output:

```
|Febins-MacBook-Air:SendCheck febinjohnjames$ ./node_modules/.bin/babel-node send_check.js
Connected to the test network.
Transaction JSON: {"Account":"r41sFTd4rftxY1VCn5ZDDipb4KaV5VLFy2","TransactionType":"CheckCreate","Destination":"r42Qv8NwggeMWnpKcxMkx7qTtB23
GYLHBX","SendMax":"100000000","Flags":2147483648,"LastLedgerSequence":15249306,"Fee":"12","Sequence":56}
Transaction Signed.
{ resultCode: 'tesSUCCESS',
  resultMessage: 'The transaction was applied. Only final in a validated ledger.',
  engine_result: 'tesSUCCESS',
  engine_result_code: 0,
  engine_result_message: 'The transaction was applied. Only final in a validated ledger.',
  tx_blob: '120010228000000002400000003820 1B00E8AF9A6840000000000000000C69400000005F5E10073210247A93474AFDBA3962177E92624843403C99A8E8B46B56430F
FB4AEA9212DB69274473045022100A2B9F3A020613DF76B2B691F2E99BDFD1D2A61A55CB49627C74F1C98AF0EB71602205AE6E56E9614E39C28B23DBE314CA4B4E08D7309EF90
DE8C0E6657E64E80D5DA8114EFD1CAC7F8FC974342DED53BD4B1A8EDDEFD3A5E8314ECAC57766694E4FA7A00C5D1C1BEFC8E4D4CE1EA',
  tx_json:
   { Account: 'r41sFTd4rftxY1VCn5ZDDipb4KaV5VLFy2',
     Destination: 'r42Qv8NwggeMWnpKcxMkx7qTtB23GYLHBX',
     Fee: '12',
     Flags: 2147483648,
     LastLedgerSequence: 15249306,
     SendMax: '100000000',
     Sequence: 56,
     SigningPubKey: '0247A93474AFDBA3962177E92624843403C99A8E8B46B56430FFB4AEA9212DB692',
     TransactionType: 'CheckCreate',
     TxnSignature: '3045022100A2B9F3A020613DF76B2B691F2E99BDFD1D2A61A55CB49627C74F1C98AF0EB71602205AE6E56E9614E39C28B23DBE314CA4B4E08D7309EF9
0DE8C0E6657E64E80D5DA',
     hash: 'AB76FF89F9B770CBA61BA719FC479AF88A54D7D05568C7306A16E75E1E06C3BA' } }
Transaction Successfully Submitted.
CheckID: 25B092AEB7966D572A0DC7BD1EFC9932F1BE081FD1F153C556132E1AAB45D153
Disconnected from test network.
```

Make a note of the check ID, as we'll be using it later in this chapter to cash the check. If you have noticed, no money has been deducted from our account. The money is only deducted when someone cashes the check.

Now, let's build a web app that allows users to log in and create checks.

In this app, we'll be using a few npm packages, hence we need browserify to compile these dependencies into one file. You can install browserify with the following command:

```
npm install -g browserify
```

We would be using the same modal we used for sending money. In this application, we'll be separating the JavaScript to a different file, app.js, so that we can use browserify to get all of the dependencies to one file:

```javascript
const RippleAPI = require('ripple-lib').RippleAPI;
const decodeAddress = require('ripple-address-codec').decodeAddress;
const createHash = require('crypto').createHash;

var api = new RippleAPI({server:'wss://s.altnet.rippletest.net:51233'});
var fetchBalance;
  $('document').ready(function(){
    login();
    $('.progress').hide();
    $('#sendCheckButton').click(function(){
        showsendCheckModal();
```

```
    });
    $('#logoutButton').click(function(){
        logout();
    });
    $("#loginButton").click(function(){
        storeCredentials();
    });
    $("#createCheckButton").click(function(){
        createCheck();
    });
});

function login(){
    if(!localStorage.getItem("loggedIn")){
        $('#loginModal').modal('show');
    } else{
        updateAccount();
    }
}

function logout(){
    localStorage.clear();
    clearInterval(fetchBalance);
    location.reload();
}

function updateAccount(){
    $('#rippleAddress').text(localStorage.getItem('rippleAddress'));
    updateBalance();
}

function storeCredentials(){
    localStorage.setItem("rippleAddress", $('#inputRippleAddress').val());
    localStorage.setItem("secret", $('#inputSecret').val());
    localStorage.setItem("loggedIn", true);
    $('#loginModal').modal('hide');
    updateAccount();
}

$("form").submit(function(e) {
    e.preventDefault();
});

function updateBalance(){
    api.connect().then(() => {
        const accountAddress = localStorage.getItem("rippleAddress");
        return api.getAccountInfo(accountAddress);
    }).then(info => {
```

```
      $('#balance').text("Account Balance : " + info.xrpBalance+ " XRP");
    }).then(() => {
      return api.disconnect();
    }).catch(console.error);
  }

  function showsendCheckModal(){
    $('#sendCheckModal').modal('show');
  }

  function createCheck(){
    $('.progress').show();
    const instructions = {};
    const sourceAddress = localStorage.getItem('rippleAddress');
    const sourceSecret = localStorage.getItem('secret');
    const destinationAddress = $('#inputDestinationRippleAddress').val();
    const options = {};

    api.connect().then(() => {

    return api.prepareCheckCreate(sourceAddress, {
          "destination": destinationAddress,
          "sendMax": {
            "currency": "XRP",
            "value": "100"
          }
        }, options).then(prepared => {
        $('.progress-bar').css('width', 40+'%').attr('aria-valuenow', 40);
        const {signedTransaction} = api.sign(prepared.txJSON,
sourceSecret);
        api.submit(signedTransaction).then(onSuccess,onFailure);
      });
    });
  }

  function calculateCheckID(transaction){
    const checkIDhasher = createHash('sha512');
    checkIDhasher.update(Buffer.from('0043', 'hex'));
    checkIDhasher.update(new
Buffer(decodeAddress(localStorage.getItem('rippleAddress'))));
    const seqBuf = Buffer.alloc(4);
    seqBuf.writeUInt32BE(transaction['tx_json']['Sequence'], 0);
    checkIDhasher.update(seqBuf);
    const checkID = checkIDhasher.digest('hex').slice(0,64).toUpperCase();
    $('#checkOutput').text("Check ID : "+checkID);
  }

  function onSuccess(message){
```

```
  $('.progress-bar').css('width', 100+'%').attr('aria-valuenow', 100);
  bootstrap_alert.success('Transaction Submitted Successfully');
  calculateCheckID(message);
  clear();
}

function onFailure(message){
  $('.progress-bar').css('width', 100+'%').attr('aria-valuenow', 100);
  bootstrap_alert.danger('Transaction Submission Failed');
  clear();
}

function clear(){
  disconnect();
  $('#sendCheckModal').modal('hide');
  $('.progress-bar').css('width', 0+'%').attr('aria-valuenow', 0);
  $(".progress").hide();
}

function disconnect(){
  api.disconnect().then(()=> {
  })
}

bootstrap_alert = function() {}

bootstrap_alert.success = function(message) {
  $('#alert').html('<div role="alert" id="success-alert" class="alert
alert-success"><p>'+message+'</p></div>');
  $("#success-alert").fadeTo(2000, 500).slideUp(500, function(){
    $("#success-alert").slideUp(500);
  });
}
bootstrap_alert.danger = function(message) {
  $('#alert').html('<div role="alert" id="danger-alert" class="alert
alert-danger"><p>'+message+'</p></div>');
  $("#danger-alert").fadeTo(2000, 500).slideUp(500, function(){
  $("#danger-alert").slideUp(500);
});
}
```

Save this file as `app.js`. Now let's use the following command to bundle all dependencies to one file:

```
browserify app.js -o bundle.js
```

Make sure, these files are save in the `js` folder. Let's now have a look at the HTML code; we've made some modifications:

```
<!DOCTYPE html>
<html>
<title> Send Check </title>
<head>
  <link rel="stylesheet" href="css/bootstrap.min.css">
</head>
<body>

<nav class="navbar navbar-expand-lg navbar-dark bg-dark">
  <a class="navbar-brand" href="#">Send Check</a>
</nav>

<br/><br/><br/>

<center>
  <p class="lead">Ripple Address : <span id="rippleAddress"> </span> </p>
  <p id="balance"> Please wait, fetching account details...</p>
  <button id="sendCheckButton" class="btn btn-primary">Send Check</button>
  <button id="logoutButton" class="btn btn-primary">Logout</button>
  <br/>
  <br/>
  <br/>
  <div id="checkOutput"> </div>
  <div id="alert" style="width:30%"></div>
</center>

<div class="modal fade" id="loginModal" tabindex="-1" role="dialog" aria-
labelledby="loginModalLabel" aria-hidden="true">
  <div class="modal-dialog" role="document">
    <div class="modal-content">
      <div class="modal-header">
        <h5 class="modal-title" id="loginModalLabel">Login</h5>
        <button type="button" class="close" data-dismiss="modal" aria-
label="Close">
          <span aria-hidden="true">&times;</span>
        </button>
      </div>
      <div class="modal-body">
        <form>
        <div class="form-group">
          <label for="inputRippleAddress">Ripple Address</label>
          <input type="text" class="form-control" id="inputRippleAddress"
aria-describedby="rippleAddressHelp" placeholder="Enter Ripple Address">
        </div>
        <div class="form-group">
```

```
            <label for="inputSecret">Secret</label>
            <input type="password" class="form-control" id="inputSecret"
placeholder="Secret">
        </div>

        <button id="loginButton" class="btn btn-primary">Login</button>
      </form>
      </div>

    </div>
  </div>
</div>

<div class="modal fade" id="sendCheckModal" tabindex="-1" role="dialog"
aria-labelledby="sendCheckModalLabel" aria-hidden="true">
  <div class="modal-dialog" role="document">
    <div class="modal-content">
      <div class="modal-header">
        <h5 class="modal-title" id="sendCheckModalLabel">Send Check </h5>
        <button type="button" class="close" data-dismiss="modal" aria-
label="Close">
          <span aria-hidden="true">&times;</span>
        </button>
      </div>
      <div class="modal-body">
        <form>
        <div class="form-group">
          <label for="inputDestinationRippleAddress">Ripple Address</label>
          <input type="text" class="form-control"
id="inputDestinationRippleAddress" aria-
describedby="destinationRippleAddressHelp" placeholder="Destination Ripple
Address">
        </div>
        <div class="form-group">
          <label for="inputAmount">Amount</label>
          <input type="number" class="form-control" id="inputAmount"
placeholder="Amount">
        </div>

        <button id="createCheckButton" class="btn btn-primary">Create
Check</button>
        <br/> <br/>
        <div class="progress">
        <div class="progress-bar progress-bar-striped bg-info"
role="progressbar" style="width: 0%" aria-valuenow="0" aria-valuemin="0"
aria-valuemax="100"></div>
        </div>
      </form>
```

```
      </div>

    </div>
  </div>
</div>

</body>

<script src="js/jquery.min.js"></script>
<script src="js/bootstrap.min.js"></script>
<script src="js/bundle.js"></script>
</html>
```

Save this file as `send_check.html`. You can now open the file in the browser to create a check:

1. Once you login you should be able to see the **Send Check** button as shown in the following screenshot:

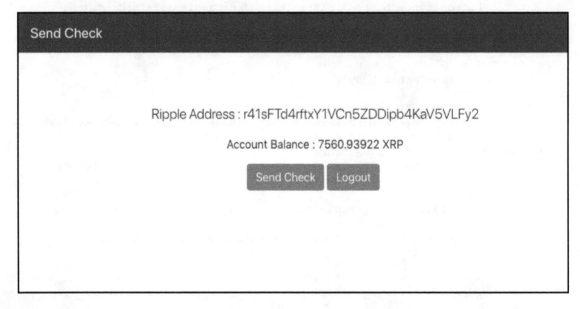

2. Once you click on the **Send Check** button, you'll be asked to fill the destination address and the check amount:

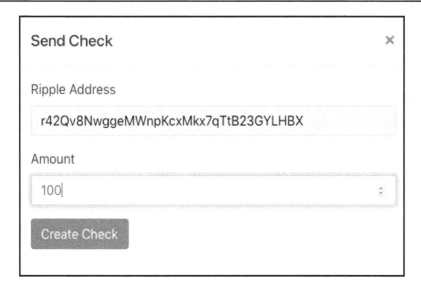

3. If everything goes well, the transaction will be submitted successfully and a check ID will be created:

4. Make a note of the check ID; we'll be using it later to cash the check. This is the second check ID you should making note of.

Great job! In the next section, we'll learn how to cash this check.

Cashing checks

You should be familiar with the process by now. It's similar to sending money and creating checks. In order to cash a check, you need to have the check ID created by the sender using the following steps:

1. **Prepare transaction**: Here we define the check ID, amount to be cashed out, and so on.
2. **Sign transaction:** You need to sign the transaction cryptographically with your secret key. This proves that you own this account.
3. **Submit transaction:** Once you sign the transaction, you need to submit it to the Ripple network for validation. The check will be cashed out and the account balance will only be updated when the validators approve your transaction.

The following code uses the `"CheckCash"` method to prepare the transaction. The sign and submit method are similar to the one we used before. We have used the check ID that we noted down earlier. You'll need to replace the check ID with the one you noted earlier. Please note, here the sender will be the recipient of the send check transaction:

```
const sender = 'r42Qv8NwggeMWnpKcxMkx7qTtB23GYLHBX';
const secret = 'shMrNknuQCteaNE3XUMEBgWs1EebU';
api.prepareCheckCash(sender, {
    "checkID":
"25B092AEB7966D572A0DC7BD1EFC9932F1BE081FD1F153C556132E1AAB45D153",
    "amount": {
        "currency": "XRP",
        "value": "100" // Cash for exactly 95 XRP
    }
}, options);
const {signedTransaction} = api.sign(prepared.txJSON, secret);
api.submit(signedTransaction).then(onSuccess,onFailure);
```

Let's see how we can use this code to cash the check:

```
'use strict';
const RippleAPI = require('ripple-lib').RippleAPI;
const decodeAddress = require('ripple-address-codec').decodeAddress;
const createHash = require('crypto').createHash;

const sender = 'r42Qv8NwggeMWnpKcxMkx7qTtB23GYLHBX';
const secret = 'shMrNknuQCteaNE3XUMEBgWs1EebU';
const options = {};

const api = new RippleAPI({server: 'wss://s.altnet.rippletest.net:51233'});
api.connect().then(() => {
```

```
    console.log('Connected');
    return api.prepareCheckCash(sender, {
      "checkID":
"25B092AEB7966D572A0DC7BD1EFC9932F1BE081FD1F153C556132E1AAB45D153",
      "amount": {
        "currency": "XRP",
        "value": "100"
      }
    }, options);

}).then(prepared => {
    console.log("txJSON:", prepared.txJSON);
    const {signedTransaction} = api.sign(prepared.txJSON, secret);
    api.submit(signedTransaction).then(onSuccess,onFailure);
});

function onSuccess(message){
    console.log(message);
    console.log("Transaction Successfully Submitted.");
    disconnect();
}

function onFailure(message){
    console.log("Transaction Submission Failed.");
    console.log(message);
    disconnect();
}

function disconnect(){
    api.disconnect().then(()=> {
      console.log("Disconnected from test network.")
    });
}
```

Let's run this code using the following command:

```
./node_modules/.bin/babel-node cash_check.js
```

If everything works fine, you should see the following output:

```
Febins-MacBook-Air:CashCheck febinjohnjames$ ./node_modules/.bin/babel-node cash_check.js
Connected
txJSON: {"Account":"r42Qv8NwggeMNnpKcxMkx7qTtB23GYLHBX","TransactionType":"CheckCash","CheckID":"25B092AEB7966D572A0DC7BD1EFC9932F1BE081FD1F1
53C556132E1AAB45D153","Amount":"100000000","Flags":2147483648,"LastLedgerSequence":15252069,"Fee":"12","Sequence":2}
{ resultCode: 'tesSUCCESS',
  resultMessage: 'The transaction was applied. Only final in a validated ledger.',
  engine_result: 'tesSUCCESS',
  engine_result_code: 0,
  engine_result_message: 'The transaction was applied. Only final in a validated ledger.',
  tx_blob: '1200112280000000024000000002201800E8BA65501825B092AEB79G6D572A0DC7BD1EFC9932F1BE081FD1F153C556132E1AAB45D1536140000000005F5E10068400
000000000000C732103BBFD46D3A7AC49F8FB52A50C45D2636523A562CB6D6C53E4075470DABF00DD3D7446304402201BEEC054D27B9011F705940E5E017D3ECD70BE7C540B1A
1F7379F96C8173B0DF02206C994B435CF6E764E100421FBE31BDAE55DAAF02F82D29D82023EE1EEF94F4308114ECAC57766694E4FA7A00C5D1C1BEFC8E4D4CE1EA',
  tx_json:
   { Account: 'r42Qv8NwggeMNnpKcxMkx7qTtB23GYLHBX',
     Amount: '100000000',
     CheckID: '25B092AEB79G6D572A0DC7BD1EFC9932F1BE081FD1F153C556132E1AAB45D153',
     Fee: '12',
     Flags: 2147483648,
     LastLedgerSequence: 15252069,
     Sequence: 2,
     SigningPubKey: '03BBFD46D3A7AC49F8FB52A50C45D2636523A562CB6D6C53E4075470DABF00DD3D',
     TransactionType: 'CheckCash',
     TxnSignature: '304402201BEEC054D27B9011F705940E5E017D3ECD70BE7C540B1A1F7379F96C8173B0DF02206C994B435CF6E764E100421FBE31BDAE55DAAF02F82D2
9D82023EE1EEF94F430',
     hash: 'D371C14292B3CB5DD75C4890151CD7AEED98CDD1204BE239D8F406BD5890EB0B' } }
Transaction Successfully Submitted
Disconnected from test network.
```

You can use the first app we created to check whether the check has been cashed out. Please note, a Ripple transaction takes 4-6 seconds to be confirmed.

Now, let's build a web app that'll provide the user with an interface to cash out the check.

We'll create a modal that inputs the check ID and the amount to be cashed out. Here's the code for our new modal:

```html
<div class="modal fade" id="cashCheckModal" tabindex="-1" role="dialog"
aria-labelledby="cashCheckModalLabel" aria-hidden="true">
  <div class="modal-dialog" role="document">
    <div class="modal-content">
      <div class="modal-header">
        <h5 class="modal-title" id="cashCheckModalLabel">Cash Check </h5>
        <button type="button" class="close" data-dismiss="modal" aria-
label="Close">
          <span aria-hidden="true">&times;</span>
        </button>
      </div>
      <div class="modal-body">
        <form>
        <div class="form-group">
          <label for="inputCheckId">Check ID</label>
          <input type="text" class="form-control" id="inputCheckId" aria-
describedby="inputCheckIdHelp" placeholder="Check ID">
        </div>
        <div class="form-group">
          <label for="inputAmount">Amount</label>
```

```
            <input type="number" class="form-control" id="inputAmount"
placeholder="Amount">
        </div>

        <button id="cashOutButton" class="btn btn-primary">Cash
Check</button>
        <br/> <br/>
        <div class="progress">
        <div class="progress-bar progress-bar-striped bg-info"
role="progressbar" style="width: 0%" aria-valuenow="0" aria-valuemin="0"
aria-valuemax="100"></div>
        </div>
      </form>
      </div>

    </div>
  </div>
</div>
```

Our cash check function is given in the following; it fetches values from the HTML form and uses the Ripple API to prepare, sign, and submit the transaction:

```
function cashCheck(){
    $('.progress').show();
    const instructions = {};
    const sourceAddress = localStorage.getItem('rippleAddress');
    const sourceSecret = localStorage.getItem('secret');
    const options = {};

    api.connect().then(() => {

    return api.prepareCheckCash(sourceAddress, {
      "checkID": $("#inputCheckId").val(),
      "amount": {
        "currency": "XRP",
        "value": $("#inputAmount").val()
      }
    }, options).then(prepared => {
        $('.progress-bar').css('width', 40+'%').attr('aria-valuenow', 40);
        const {signedTransaction} = api.sign(prepared.txJSON,
sourceSecret);
        api.submit(signedTransaction).then(onSuccess, onFailure);
      });
    });
}
```

When we put everything together, here's what our JavaScript code will look like:

```javascript
const RippleAPI = require('ripple-lib').RippleAPI;
const decodeAddress = require('ripple-address-codec').decodeAddress;
const createHash = require('crypto').createHash;

var api = new RippleAPI({server:'wss://s.altnet.rippletest.net:51233'});
var fetchBalance;
$('document').ready(function(){
  login();
  $('.progress').hide();
  $('#cashCheckButton').click(function(){
      showCashCheckModal();
  });
  $('#logoutButton').click(function(){
      logout();
  });
  $("#loginButton").click(function(){
      storeCredentials();
  });
  $("#cashOutButton").click(function(){
    cashCheck();
  });
});

function login(){
  if(!localStorage.getItem("loggedIn")){
    $('#loginModal').modal('show');
  } else{
    updateAccount();
  }
}

function logout(){
  localStorage.clear();
  clearInterval(fetchBalance);
  location.reload();
}

function updateAccount(){
  $('#rippleAddress').text(localStorage.getItem('rippleAddress'));
  updateBalance();
}

function storeCredentials(){
  localStorage.setItem("rippleAddress", $('#inputRippleAddress').val());
  localStorage.setItem("secret", $('#inputSecret').val());
  localStorage.setItem("loggedIn", true);
```

```javascript
    $('#loginModal').modal('hide');
    updateAccount();
  }

  $("form").submit(function(e) {
    e.preventDefault();
  });

  function updateBalance(){
    api.connect().then(() => {
      const accountAddress = localStorage.getItem("rippleAddress");
      return api.getAccountInfo(accountAddress);
    }).then(info => {
      $('#balance').text("Account Balance : " + info.xrpBalance+ " XRP");
    }).then(() => {
      return api.disconnect();
    }).catch(console.error);
  }

  function showCashCheckModal(){
    $('#cashCheckModal').modal('show');
  }

  function cashCheck(){
    $('.progress').show();
    const instructions = {};
    const sourceAddress = localStorage.getItem('rippleAddress');
    const sourceSecret = localStorage.getItem('secret');
    const options = {};

    api.connect().then(() => {

    return api.prepareCheckCash(sourceAddress, {
      "checkID": $("#inputCheckId").val(),
      "amount": {
        "currency": "XRP",
        "value": $("#inputAmount").val()
      }
    }, options).then(prepared => {
        $('.progress-bar').css('width', 40+'%').attr('aria-valuenow', 40);
        const {signedTransaction} = api.sign(prepared.txJSON,
sourceSecret);
        api.submit(signedTransaction).then(onSuccess,onFailure);
      });
    });
  }
```

```
function onSuccess(message){
  console.log(message);
  $('.progress-bar').css('width', 100+'%').attr('aria-valuenow', 100);
  bootstrap_alert.success('Transaction Submitted Successfully');
  clear();
  $('#balance').text("Fetching updated balance, please wait.");
  setTimeout(updateBalance,6000);
}

function onFailure(message){
  console.log(message);
  $('.progress-bar').css('width', 100+'%').attr('aria-valuenow', 100);
  bootstrap_alert.danger('Transaction Submission Failed');
  clear();
}

function clear(){
  disconnect();
  $('#cashCheckModal').modal('hide');
  $('.progress-bar').css('width', 0+'%').attr('aria-valuenow', 0);
  $(".progress").hide();
}

function disconnect(){
  api.disconnect().then(()=> {
  })
}

bootstrap_alert = function() {}

bootstrap_alert.success = function(message) {
  $('#alert').html('<div role="alert" id="success-alert" class="alert
alert-success"><p>'+message+'</p></div>');
  $("#success-alert").fadeTo(2000, 500).slideUp(500, function(){
    $("#success-alert").slideUp(500);
  });
}
bootstrap_alert.danger = function(message) {
  $('#alert').html('<div role="alert" id="danger-alert" class="alert
alert-danger"><p>'+message+'</p></div>');
  $("#danger-alert").fadeTo(2000, 500).slideUp(500, function(){
  $("#danger-alert").slideUp(500);
});
}
```

Save this file as `app.js`. Let's `browserify` it using the following command:

```
browserify app.js -o bundle.js
```

Make sure these files are save in the `js` directory.

Here's what our HTML code should look like:

```html
<!DOCTYPE html>
<html>
<title> Cash Check </title>
<head>
  <link rel="stylesheet" href="css/bootstrap.min.css">
</head>
<body>

<nav class="navbar navbar-expand-lg navbar-dark bg-dark">
  <a class="navbar-brand" href="#">Cash Check</a>
</nav>

<br/><br/><br/>

<center>
  <p class="lead">Ripple Address : <span id="rippleAddress"> </span> </p>
  <p id="balance"> Please wait, fetching account details...</p>
  <button id="cashCheckButton" class="btn btn-primary">Cash Check</button>
  <button id="logoutButton" class="btn btn-primary">Logout</button>
  <br/>
  <br/>
  <br/>
  <div id="checkOutput"> </div>
  <div id="alert" style="width:30%"></div>
</center>

<div class="modal fade" id="loginModal" tabindex="-1" role="dialog" aria-
labelledby="loginModalLabel" aria-hidden="true">
  <div class="modal-dialog" role="document">
    <div class="modal-content">
      <div class="modal-header">
        <h5 class="modal-title" id="loginModalLabel">Login</h5>
        <button type="button" class="close" data-dismiss="modal" aria-
label="Close">
          <span aria-hidden="true">&times;</span>
        </button>
      </div>
      <div class="modal-body">
        <form>
        <div class="form-group">
```

```
          <label for="inputRippleAddress">Ripple Address</label>
          <input type="text" class="form-control" id="inputRippleAddress"
aria-describedby="rippleAddressHelp" placeholder="Enter Ripple Address">
        </div>
        <div class="form-group">
          <label for="inputSecret">Secret</label>
          <input type="password" class="form-control" id="inputSecret"
placeholder="Secret">
        </div>

          <button id="loginButton" class="btn btn-primary">Login</button>
      </form>
      </div>

    </div>
  </div>
</div>

<div class="modal fade" id="cashCheckModal" tabindex="-1" role="dialog"
aria-labelledby="cashCheckModalLabel" aria-hidden="true">
  <div class="modal-dialog" role="document">
    <div class="modal-content">
      <div class="modal-header">
        <h5 class="modal-title" id="cashCheckModalLabel">Cash Check </h5>
        <button type="button" class="close" data-dismiss="modal" aria-
label="Close">
          <span aria-hidden="true">&times;</span>
        </button>
      </div>
      <div class="modal-body">
        <form>
        <div class="form-group">
          <label for="inputCheckId">Check ID</label>
          <input type="text" class="form-control" id="inputCheckId" aria-
describedby="inputCheckIdHelp" placeholder="Check ID">
        </div>
        <div class="form-group">
          <label for="inputAmount">Amount</label>
          <input type="number" class="form-control" id="inputAmount"
placeholder="Amount">
        </div>

          <button id="cashOutButton" class="btn btn-primary">Cash
Check</button>
          <br/> <br/>
          <div class="progress">
          <div class="progress-bar progress-bar-striped bg-info"
role="progressbar" style="width: 0%" aria-valuenow="0" aria-valuemin="0"
```

```
aria-valuemax="100"></div>
        </div>
      </form>
      </div>

    </div>
   </div>
</div>

</body>

<script src="js/jquery.min.js"></script>
<script src="js/bootstrap.min.js"></script>
<script src="js/bundle.js"></script>
</html>
```

Save this as `cash_check.html`. We can now run this file on a browser. The home page should look like the following:

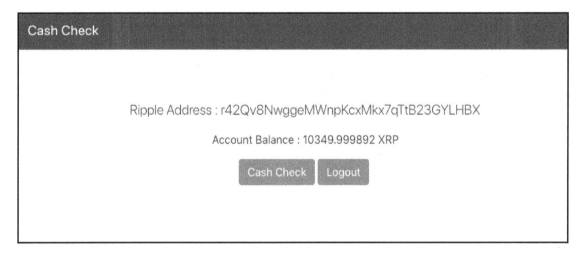

In the **Cash Check** form, we'll input the check ID we made note of earlier. We'll also enter the amount that should be cashed out, as shown in the following screenshot:

If everything works fine, your check will be successfully cashed out and your account balance will be updated:

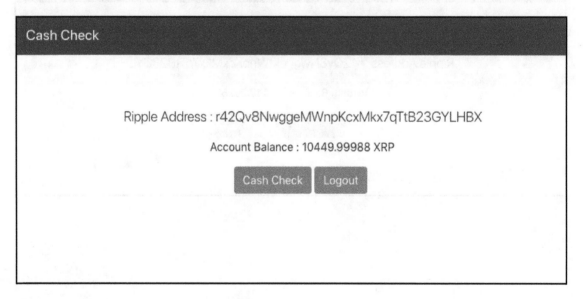

Great work! We've now learned how to send and cash out checks on Ripple.

Creating a time-held escrow

We'll again go with the same step of steps as before to create a time-held escrow:

1. **Prepare transaction**: Here, we define the destination account to which money should be released, escrow release time, amount, and so on.
2. **Sign transaction:** You need to sign the transaction cryptographically with your secret key. This proves that you own the source account.
3. **Submit transaction:** Once you sign the transaction, you need to submit it to the Ripple network for validation. The escrow would be only created when the validators approve the transaction.

We prepare the create escrow transaction with the following code. As you can see, we've defined the destination and amount and passed the release time to `"allowExecuteAfter"` parameter:

```
const sender = 'r41sFTd4rftxY1VCn5ZDDipb4KaV5VLFy2';
const secret = 'sptkAoSPzHq8mKLWrjU33EDj7v96u';
const options = {};
const release_date = new Date("2018-12-16T14:10:00Z");

const api = new RippleAPI({server: 'wss://s.altnet.rippletest.net:51233'});
api.connect().then(() => {
  console.log('Connected');
  return api.prepareEscrowCreation(sender, {
      "destination": "r42Qv8NwggeMWnpKcxMkx7qTtB23GYLHBX",
      "amount": '50',
      "allowExecuteAfter": release_date.toISOString()
  }, options);
```

Later, we sign and submit the transaction to the network using the following code:

```
const {signedTransaction} = api.sign(prepared.txJSON, secret);
api.submit(signedTransaction).then(onSuccess,onFailure);
```

Now, let's put everything together and see what the code looks like. You'll need to change the time to somewhere in the near future since you'll also be writing code to release the same escrow. Remember, the escrow cannot be released until the release time is passed:

```
'use strict';
const RippleAPI = require('ripple-lib').RippleAPI;

const sender = 'r41sFTd4rftxY1VCn5ZDDipb4KaV5VLFy2';
const secret = 'sptkAoSPzHq8mKLWrjU33EDj7v96u';
const options = {};
const release_date = new Date("2018-12-16T14:10:00Z");
```

```
const api = new RippleAPI({server: 'wss://s.altnet.rippletest.net:51233'});
api.connect().then(() => {
  console.log('Connected');
  return api.prepareEscrowCreation(sender, {
      "destination": "r42Qv8NwggeMWnpKcxMkx7qTtB23GYLHBX",
      "amount": '50',
      "allowExecuteAfter": release_date.toISOString()
  }, options);

}).then(prepared => {
  console.log("txJSON:", prepared.txJSON);
  const {signedTransaction} = api.sign(prepared.txJSON, secret);
  api.submit(signedTransaction).then(onSuccess,onFailure);
});

function onSuccess(message){
  console.log(message);
  console.log("Transaction Successfully Submitted.");
  disconnect();
}

function onFailure(message){
  console.log("Transaction Submission Failed.");
  console.log(message);
  disconnect();
}

function disconnect(){
  api.disconnect().then(()=> {
    console.log("Disconnected from test network.")
  });
}
```

Save this to a file and name it escrow_create.js.

Let's run the code using the following command:

```
./node_modules/.bin/babel-node escrow_release.js
```

If everything goes well, the following output will be displayed:

```
Febins-MacBook-Air:TimeEscrow febinjohnjames$ ./node_modules/.bin/babel-node escrow_create.js
Connected
txJSON: {"TransactionType":"EscrowCreate","Account":"r41sFTd4rftxY1VCn5ZDDipb4KaV5VLFy2","Destination":"r42Qv8NwggeMWnpKcxMkx7qTtB23GYLHBX","
Amount":"50000000","FinishAfter":598284600,"Flags":2147483648,"LastLedgerSequence":15255215,"Fee":"12","Sequence":67}
{ resultCode: 'tesSUCCESS',
  resultMessage: 'The transaction was applied. Only final in a validated ledger.',
  engine_result: 'tesSUCCESS',
  engine_result_code: 0,
  engine_result_message: 'The transaction was applied. Only final in a validated ledger.',
  tx_blob: '12000122800000002400000043201800E8C6AF202523A919386140000000002FAF08068400000000000000C73210247A93474AFDBA3962177E92624843403C99A8
E8B46B56430FFB4AEA9212DB69274463044022063 0AD72A34B385A9704579C45EB2A2C0962CB80E01085771ED0BED9F2DC2EE2D02207705645DBE7C8DA4359E0881084F381A7C
ADB87286835019A3302E78E1347C078114EFD1CAC7F8FC974342DED53BD4B1ABEDDEFD3A5E8314ECAC57766694E4FA7A00C5D1C1BEFC8E4D4CE1EA',
  tx_json:
  { Account: 'r41sFTd4rftxY1VCn5ZDDipb4KaV5VLFy2',
    Amount: '50000000',
    Destination: 'r42Qv8NwggeMWnpKcxMkx7qTtB23GYLHBX',
    Fee: '12',
    FinishAfter: 598284600,
    Flags: 2147483648,
    LastLedgerSequence: 15255215,
    Sequence: 67,
    SigningPubKey: '0247A93474AFDBA3962177E92624843403C99A8E8B46B56430FFB4AEA9212DB692',
    TransactionType: 'EscrowCreate',
    TxnSignature: '304402206630AD72A34B385A9704579C45EB2A2C0962CB80E01085771ED0BED9F2DC2EE2D02207705645DBE7C8DA4359E0881084F381A7CADB87286835
019A3302E78E1347C07',
    hash: '9F202440C0072ACF840C95A18CBE567680360765162C2A60A28724423CB3E9E3' } }
Transaction Successfully Submitted.
Disconnected from test network.
```

You've successfully created the escrow. Make a note of the `sequence` parameter in the output; we'll be using it to release the escrow. Now, in order to release the escrow, we need to follow the same three steps that're given in the following:

1. **Prepare transaction**: Here, we define the owner account that created the escrow and the sequence parameter we received from escrow creation.
2. **Sign transaction:** Escrow can be signed by anyone. However, the release amount will only go to the designated account specified during the creation of the escrow.
3. **Submit transaction:** Once you sign the transaction, you need to submit it to the Ripple network for validation. The escrow will only be released when the validators approve the transaction.

Here's the code to prepare, sign, and submit the `"escrowFinish"` transaction. Please note in the code that's given below, the owner of the escrow is releasing it, hence the owner and sender are the same address. However, this need not be the case—anyone can release an escrow. You'll need to replace this `"escrowSequence"` parameter:

```
api.prepareEscrowExecution(sender, {
    "owner": sender,
    "escrowSequence": 67,
}, options);

const {signedTransaction} = api.sign(prepared.txJSON, secret);
api.submit(signedTransaction).then(onSuccess,onFailure);
```

Let's use the following code to connect to the Ripple network and release the escrow:

```
'use strict';
const RippleAPI = require('ripple-lib').RippleAPI;


const sender = 'r41sFTd4rftxY1VCn5ZDDipb4KaV5VLFy2';
const secret = 'sptkAoSPzHq8mKLWrjU33EDj7v96u';
const options = {};
const release_date = new Date("2018-12-16T14:10:00Z");

const api = new RippleAPI({server: 'wss://s.altnet.rippletest.net:51233'});
api.connect().then(() => {
  console.log('Connected');
  return api.prepareEscrowExecution(sender, {
      "owner": sender,
      "escrowSequence": 67,
  }, options);

}).then(prepared => {
  console.log("txJSON:", prepared.txJSON);
  const {signedTransaction} = api.sign(prepared.txJSON, secret);
  api.submit(signedTransaction).then(onSuccess,onFailure);
});

function onSuccess(message){
  console.log(message);
  console.log("Transaction Successfully Submitted.");
  disconnect();
}

function onFailure(message){
  console.log("Transaction Submission Failed.");
  console.log(message);
  disconnect();
}

function disconnect(){
  api.disconnect().then(()=> {
    console.log("Disconnected from test network.")
  });
}
```

Save this file as `escrow_release.js`. Let's run the code by using the following command:

```
./node_modules/.bin/babel-node escrow_release.js
```

Please note, this code would only work if the escrow release time mentioned during the time of creation has passed. Otherwise, you'll receive a permission error.

If everything goes well, the following output will be displayed:

```
Connected
txJSON: {"TransactionType":"EscrowFinish","Account":"r41sFTd4rftxY1VCn5ZDDipb4KaV5VLFy2","Owner":"r41sFTd4rftxY1VCn5ZDDipb4KaV5VLFy2","OfferS
equence":67,"Flags":2147483648,"LastLedgerSequence":15255401,"Fee":"12","Sequence":70}
{ resultCode: 'tesSUCCESS',
  resultMessage: 'The transaction was applied. Only final in a validated ledger.',
  engine_result: 'tesSUCCESS',
  engine_result_code: 0,
  engine_result_message: 'The transaction was applied. Only final in a validated ledger.',
  tx_blob: '1200022280000000240000004620190000000043201B00E8C769684000000000000000C73210247A93474AFDBA3962177E92624843403C99A8E8B46B56430FFB4AEA
9212DB6927447304502210008107AC83507C3326415F804E61B55C1DD2BC00F52BB41B770C6087ED12855FFC02200F5C3A92BE4F010938D81CD1617E9BE827CBCAD9C191384254
3F5EEF47297E9A8114EFD1CAC7F8FC974342DED53BD4B1ABEDDEFD3A5E8214EFD1CAC7F8FC974342DED53BD4B1ABEDDEFD3A5E',
  tx_json:
   { Account: 'r41sFTd4rftxY1VCn5ZDDipb4KaV5VLFy2',
     Fee: '12',
     Flags: 2147483648,
     LastLedgerSequence: 15255401,
     OfferSequence: 67,
     Owner: 'r41sFTd4rftxY1VCn5ZDDipb4KaV5VLFy2',
     Sequence: 70,
     SigningPubKey: '0247A93474AFDBA3962177E92624843403C99A8E8B46B56430FFB4AEA9212DB692',
     TransactionType: 'EscrowFinish',
     TxnSignature: '304502210008107AC83507C3326415F804E61B55C1DD2BC00F52BB41B770C6087ED12855FFC02200F5C3A92BE4F010938D81CD1617E9BE827CBCAD9C19
13842543F5EEF47297E9A',
     hash: 'B70E51A65F789F390F852ED3CED26C660BC79DEE04BB652F3833A0ADAC0B88B4' } }
Transaction Successfully Submitted.
Disconnected from test network.
```

Once the validators confirm the transaction, the destination account will be credited with the escrow amount. Let's now see how we can use this code to build a web app that'll allow users to easily create time-held escrows.

We'll need two forms, one to create the escrow and another to release it.

Here's the code that inputs the necessary fields to create an escrow:

```
<div class="modal fade" id="createEscrowModal" tabindex="-1" role="dialog"
aria-labelledby="createEscrowModalLabel" aria-hidden="true">
  <div class="modal-dialog" role="document">
    <div class="modal-content">
      <div class="modal-header">
        <h5 class="modal-title" id="createEscrowModalLabel">Create Escrow
</h5>
        <button type="button" class="close" data-dismiss="modal" aria-
label="Close">
          <span aria-hidden="true">&times;</span>
        </button>
      </div>
      <div class="modal-body">
        <form>
        <div class="form-group">
          <label for="inputDestinationAddress">Destination</label>
          <input type="text" class="form-control"
```

```
         id="inputDestinationAddress" aria-describedby="inputDestinationAddressHelp"
placeholder="Destination Address">
          </div>
          <div class="form-group">
            <label for="inputAmount">Amount</label>
            <input type="number" class="form-control" id="inputAmount"
placeholder="Amount">
          </div>
          <div class="form-group">
            <label for="inputDate">Release Date (UTC)</label>
            <input type="date" class="form-control" id="inputDate"
placeholder="Date">
          </div>
            <div class="form-group">
              <label for="inputTime">Release Time (UTC)</label>
              <input type="time" class="form-control" id="inputTime"
placeholder="Time">
            </div>

            <button id="createEscrowButton" class="btn btn-primary">Create
Escrow</button>
            <br/> <br/>
            <div class="progress">
            <div class="progress-bar progress-bar-striped bg-info"
role="progressbar" style="width: 0%" aria-valuenow="0" aria-valuemin="0"
aria-valuemax="100"></div>
            </div>
        </form>
        </div>

      </div>
   </div>
</div>
```

Here's the code to the form that takes input to release an escrow:

```
<div class="modal fade" id="releaseEscrowModal" tabindex="-1" role="dialog"
aria-labelledby="releaseEscrowModalLabel" aria-hidden="true">
   <div class="modal-dialog" role="document">
      <div class="modal-content">
        <div class="modal-header">
          <h5 class="modal-title" id="releaseEscrowModalLabel">Release Escrow
</h5>
          <button type="button" class="close" data-dismiss="modal" aria-
label="Close">
            <span aria-hidden="true">&times;</span>
          </button>
        </div>
```

```html
        <div class="modal-body">
          <form>
          <div class="form-group">
            <label for="inputOwnerAddress">Owner</label>
            <input type="text" class="form-control" id="inputOwnerAddress"
aria-describedby="inputOwnerAddressHelp" placeholder="Owner Address">
          </div>
          <div class="form-group">
            <label for="inputSequence">Sequence</label>
            <input type="number" class="form-control" id="inputSequence"
placeholder="Sequence">
          </div>

          <button id="releaseEscrowButton" class="btn btn-primary">Release
Escrow</button>
          <br/> <br/>
          <div class="progress">
          <div class="progress-bar progress-bar-striped bg-info"
role="progressbar" style="width: 0%" aria-valuenow="0" aria-valuemin="0"
aria-valuemax="100"></div>
          </div>
        </form>
        </div>

      </div>
    </div>
</div>
```

On the JavaScript code, we've added two functions, one to create an and another to release it:

```javascript
function createEscrow(){
    $('.progress').show();
    const instructions = {};
    const sourceAddress = localStorage.getItem('rippleAddress');
    const sourceSecret = localStorage.getItem('secret');
    const releaseDateTime = new
Date($("#inputDate").val()+"T"+$("#inputTime").val()+"Z");
    const options = {};

    api.connect().then(() => {

    return api.prepareEscrowCreation(sourceAddress, {
        "destination": $("#inputDestinationAddress").val(),
        "amount": $("#inputAmount").val(),
        "allowExecuteAfter": releaseDateTime.toISOString()
    }, options).then(prepared => {
        $('.progress-bar').css('width', 40+'%').attr('aria-valuenow', 40);
```

```
            const {signedTransaction} = api.sign(prepared.txJSON,
sourceSecret);
            api.submit(signedTransaction).then(onSuccess,onFailure);
        });
    });
  }

  function releaseEscrow(){
      $('.progress').show();
      const instructions = {};
      const sourceAddress = localStorage.getItem('rippleAddress');
      const sourceSecret = localStorage.getItem('secret');
      const options = {};

      api.connect().then(() => {

      return api.prepareEscrowExecution(sourceAddress, {
          "owner": $("#inputOwnerAddress").val(),
          "escrowSequence": parseInt($("#inputSequence").val()),
      }, options).then(prepared => {
          $('.progress-bar').css('width', 40+'%').attr('aria-valuenow',
40);
          const {signedTransaction} = api.sign(prepared.txJSON,
sourceSecret);
          api.submit(signedTransaction).then(onSuccessRelease,onFailure);
        });
      });
    }
```

When we put together our HTML code, here's what it should look like:

```
<!DOCTYPE html>
<html>
<title> Time Escrow </title>
<head>
  <link rel="stylesheet" href="css/bootstrap.min.css">
</head>
<body>

<nav class="navbar navbar-expand-lg navbar-dark bg-dark">
  <a class="navbar-brand" href="#">Time Escrow</a>
</nav>

<br/><br/><br/>

<center>
  <p class="lead">Ripple Address : <span id="rippleAddress"> </span> </p>
  <p id="balance"> Please wait, fetching account details...</p>
```

```
    <button id="showCreateEscrowButton" class="btn btn-primary">Create Time-
Held Escrow</button>
      <button id="showReleaseEscrowButton" class="btn btn-primary">Release
Escrow</button>

    <button id="logoutButton" class="btn btn-primary">Logout</button>
    <br/>
    <br/>
    <br/>
    <div id="escrowOutput"> </div>
    <div id="alert" style="width:30%"></div>
</center>

<div class="modal fade" id="loginModal" tabindex="-1" role="dialog" aria-
labelledby="loginModalLabel" aria-hidden="true">
  <div class="modal-dialog" role="document">
    <div class="modal-content">
      <div class="modal-header">
        <h5 class="modal-title" id="loginModalLabel">Login</h5>
        <button type="button" class="close" data-dismiss="modal" aria-
label="Close">
          <span aria-hidden="true">&times;</span>
        </button>
      </div>
      <div class="modal-body">
        <form>
        <div class="form-group">
          <label for="inputRippleAddress">Ripple Address</label>
          <input type="text" class="form-control" id="inputRippleAddress"
aria-describedby="rippleAddressHelp" placeholder="Enter Ripple Address">
        </div>
        <div class="form-group">
          <label for="inputSecret">Secret</label>
          <input type="password" class="form-control" id="inputSecret"
placeholder="Secret">
        </div>

        <button id="loginButton" class="btn btn-primary">Login</button>
      </form>
      </div>

    </div>
  </div>
</div>

<div class="modal fade" id="createEscrowModal" tabindex="-1" role="dialog"
aria-labelledby="createEscrowModalLabel" aria-hidden="true">
  <div class="modal-dialog" role="document">
```

```
      <div class="modal-content">
        <div class="modal-header">
          <h5 class="modal-title" id="createEscrowModalLabel">Create Escrow
</h5>
          <button type="button" class="close" data-dismiss="modal" aria-
label="Close">
            <span aria-hidden="true">&times;</span>
          </button>
        </div>
        <div class="modal-body">
          <form>
          <div class="form-group">
            <label for="inputDestinationAddress">Destination</label>
            <input type="text" class="form-control"
id="inputDestinationAddress" aria-describedby="inputDestinationAddressHelp"
placeholder="Destination Address">
          </div>
          <div class="form-group">
            <label for="inputAmount">Amount</label>
            <input type="number" class="form-control" id="inputAmount"
placeholder="Amount">
          </div>
          <div class="form-group">
            <label for="inputDate">Release Date (UTC)</label>
            <input type="date" class="form-control" id="inputDate"
placeholder="Date">
          </div>
            <div class="form-group">
              <label for="inputTime">Release Time (UTC)</label>
              <input type="time" class="form-control" id="inputTime"
placeholder="Time">
            </div>

          <button id="createEscrowButton" class="btn btn-primary">Create
Escrow</button>
          <br/> <br/>
          <div class="progress">
          <div class="progress-bar progress-bar-striped bg-info"
role="progressbar" style="width: 0%" aria-valuenow="0" aria-valuemin="0"
aria-valuemax="100"></div>
          </div>
        </form>
        </div>

      </div>
    </div>
</div>
```

```html
<div class="modal fade" id="releaseEscrowModal" tabindex="-1" role="dialog"
aria-labelledby="releaseEscrowModalLabel" aria-hidden="true">
  <div class="modal-dialog" role="document">
    <div class="modal-content">
      <div class="modal-header">
        <h5 class="modal-title" id="releaseEscrowModalLabel">Release Escrow
</h5>
        <button type="button" class="close" data-dismiss="modal" aria-
label="Close">
          <span aria-hidden="true">&times;</span>
        </button>
      </div>
      <div class="modal-body">
        <form>
        <div class="form-group">
          <label for="inputOwnerAddress">Owner</label>
          <input type="text" class="form-control" id="inputOwnerAddress"
aria-describedby="inputOwnerAddressHelp" placeholder="Owner Address">
        </div>
        <div class="form-group">
          <label for="inputSequence">Sequence</label>
          <input type="number" class="form-control" id="inputSequence"
placeholder="Sequence">
        </div>

        <button id="releaseEscrowButton" class="btn btn-primary">Release
Escrow</button>
        <br/> <br/>
        <div class="progress">
        <div class="progress-bar progress-bar-striped bg-info"
role="progressbar" style="width: 0%" aria-valuenow="0" aria-valuemin="0"
aria-valuemax="100"></div>
        </div>
      </form>
      </div>

    </div>
  </div>
</div>

</body>

<script src="js/jquery.min.js"></script>
<script src="js/bootstrap.min.js"></script>
<script src="js/bundle.js"></script>
</html>
```

Save the previous code to `escrow_create.html`. Here's what the JavaScript code should look like:

```
const RippleAPI = require('ripple-lib').RippleAPI;


var api = new RippleAPI({server:'wss://s.altnet.rippletest.net:51233'});
var fetchBalance;
$('document').ready(function(){
  login();
  $('.progress').hide();
  $('#showCreateEscrowButton').click(function(){
      showcreateEscrowModal();
  });
  $('#logoutButton').click(function(){
      logout();
  });
  $("#loginButton").click(function(){
      storeCredentials();
  });
  $("#createEscrowButton").click(function(){
    createEscrow();
  });
  $("#releaseEscrowButton").click(function(){
    releaseEscrow();
  });
  $("#showReleaseEscrowButton").click(function(){
      showReleaseEscrowModal();
  });
});

function login(){
  if(!localStorage.getItem("loggedIn")){
    $('#loginModal').modal('show');
  } else{
    updateAccount();
  }
}

function logout(){
  localStorage.clear();
  clearInterval(fetchBalance);
  location.reload();
}

function updateAccount(){
  $('#rippleAddress').text(localStorage.getItem('rippleAddress'));
  updateBalance();
```

```
  }

  function storeCredentials(){
    localStorage.setItem("rippleAddress", $('#inputRippleAddress').val());
    localStorage.setItem("secret", $('#inputSecret').val());
    localStorage.setItem("loggedIn", true);
    $('#loginModal').modal('hide');
    updateAccount();
  }

  $("form").submit(function(e) {
    e.preventDefault();
  });

  function updateBalance(){
    api.connect().then(() => {
      const accountAddress = localStorage.getItem("rippleAddress");
      return api.getAccountInfo(accountAddress);
    }).then(info => {
      $('#balance').text("Account Balance : " + info.xrpBalance+ " XRP");
    }).then(() => {
      return api.disconnect();
    }).catch(console.error);
  }

  function showcreateEscrowModal(){
    $('#createEscrowModal').modal('show');
  }

  function showReleaseEscrowModal(){
    $('#releaseEscrowModal').modal('show');
  }

  function createEscrow(){
    $('.progress').show();
    const instructions = {};
    const sourceAddress = localStorage.getItem('rippleAddress');
    const sourceSecret = localStorage.getItem('secret');
    const releaseDateTime = new
Date($("#inputDate").val()+"T"+$("#inputTime").val()+"Z");
    const options = {};

    api.connect().then(() => {

    return api.prepareEscrowCreation(sourceAddress, {
        "destination": $("#inputDestinationAddress").val(),
        "amount": $("#inputAmount").val(),
        "allowExecuteAfter": releaseDateTime.toISOString()
```

```
        }, options).then(prepared => {
            $('.progress-bar').css('width', 40+'%').attr('aria-valuenow', 40);
            const {signedTransaction} = api.sign(prepared.txJSON,
sourceSecret);
            api.submit(signedTransaction).then(onSuccess,onFailure);
        });
    });
  }

  function releaseEscrow(){
        $('.progress').show();
        const instructions = {};
        const sourceAddress = localStorage.getItem('rippleAddress');
        const sourceSecret = localStorage.getItem('secret');
        const options = {};

        api.connect().then(() => {

        return api.prepareEscrowExecution(sourceAddress, {
            "owner": $("#inputOwnerAddress").val(),
            "escrowSequence": parseInt($("#inputSequence").val()),
        }, options).then(prepared => {
            $('.progress-bar').css('width', 40+'%').attr('aria-valuenow',
40);
            const {signedTransaction} = api.sign(prepared.txJSON,
sourceSecret);
            api.submit(signedTransaction).then(onSuccessRelease,onFailure);
        });
        });
  }

  function onSuccessRelease(message){
    $('.progress-bar').css('width', 100+'%').attr('aria-valuenow', 100);
    bootstrap_alert.success('Transaction Submitted Successfully');
    clear();
  }

  function onSuccess(message){
    console.log(message);
    $('.progress-bar').css('width', 100+'%').attr('aria-valuenow', 100);
    bootstrap_alert.success('Transaction Submitted Successfully');
    $('#escrowOutput').text("Created Escrow Sequence :
"+message['tx_json']['Sequence']);
    $('#balance').text("Fetching updated balance, please wait.");
    clear();
    setTimeout(updateBalance,6000);
  }
```

```
function onFailure(message){
    console.log(message);
    $('.progress-bar').css('width', 100+'%').attr('aria-valuenow', 100);
    bootstrap_alert.danger('Transaction Submission Failed');
    clear();
}

function clear(){
    disconnect();
    $('#createEscrowModal').modal('hide');
    $('#releaseEscrowModal').modal('hide');
    $('.progress-bar').css('width', 0+'%').attr('aria-valuenow', 0);
    $(".progress").hide();
}

function disconnect(){
    api.disconnect().then(()=> {
    })
}

bootstrap_alert = function() {}

bootstrap_alert.success = function(message) {
    $('#alert').html('<div role="alert" id="success-alert" class="alert
alert-success"><p>'+message+'</p></div>');
    $("#success-alert").fadeTo(2000, 500).slideUp(500, function(){
        $("#success-alert").slideUp(500);
    });
}
bootstrap_alert.danger = function(message) {
    $('#alert').html('<div role="alert" id="danger-alert" class="alert
alert-danger"><p>'+message+'</p></div>');
    $("#danger-alert").fadeTo(2000, 500).slideUp(500, function(){
    $("#danger-alert").slideUp(500);
});
    }
```

Save the previous code to app.js. We should browserify it using the following command:

```
browserify app.js -o bundle.js
```

Make sure the created `bundle.js` is saved in the `js` directory. Let's open the HTML on a browser. If everything goes well, the following screen will be displayed:

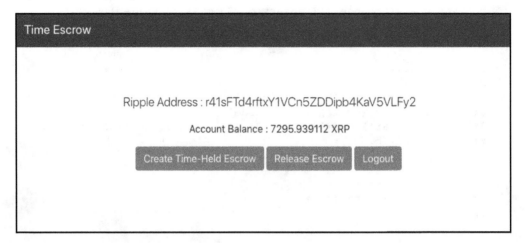

You can create the escrow by specifying the destination address, amount, and release time in UTC as shown in the following screenshot. Please select a nearby time, because you can release the escrow only when the time has lapsed:

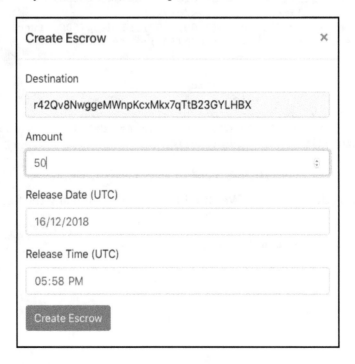

Once you create the escrow, your account balance will be deducted. The sequence will be output on the screen as shown in the following—make a note of it. We need this to release the escrow:

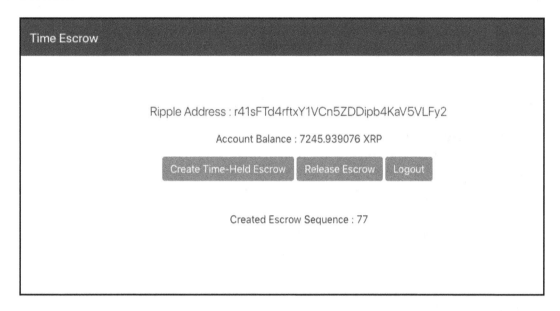

Finally, you can release the escrow using the release escrow form by inputting the sequence and the address of the owner of the escrow as shown in the following screenshot:

Once the transaction is confirmed, the destination account should be credited with the respective amount.

Great work!

You've learned how to create a time-held escrow. Now, let's learn how to create a conditionally-held escrow.

Creating a conditionally-held escrow

Conditionally-held escrows are similar to time-held escrows. However, you need to send the condition and the fulfillment after the release time for the escrow to be released. Ripple makes use of crypto conditions. For the purpose of this tutorial, we'll be generating a random fulfillment and condition. You need to keep the fulfillment secret, otherwise, anyone with the fulfillment code will be able to release the escrow.

Let's generate a random fulfillment and condition. You'll need to install the `five-bells-condition` npm library. You can do that using the following command:

```
npm install five-bells-condition
```

Use the following code to generate a random fulfillment and condition:

```javascript
const cc = require('five-bells-condition')
const crypto = require('crypto')

const preimageData = crypto.randomBytes(32);
const myFulfillment = new cc.PreimageSha256();
myFulfillment.setPreimage(preimageData);

const condition =
myFulfillment.getConditionBinary().toString('hex').toUpperCase();
console.log('Condition:', condition);

const fulfillment =
myFulfillment.serializeBinary().toString('hex').toUpperCase();
console.log('Fulfillment:', fulfillment);
```

Save this to file and name it `generate_fulfillment.js`.

You can run the code using the following command:

```
./node_modules/.bin/babel-node generate_fulfillment.js
```

You should be able to see the following output on execution of the previous command:

```
Febins-MacBook-Air:ConditionEscrow febinjohnjames$ ./node_modules/.bin/babel-node generate_fulfillment.js
Condition: A025802010BE1D1DE61FE69A9EE99689CB79820326BF6CA8A725F6631A0CE00A07B134DA810120
Fulfillment: A022802021EB4CB44AD71E3B2A23B4AAF6A546EA208960737C23F29F0645499968664404
```

Make sure you save the condition and the fulfillment. The creation process of the conditionally-held escrow is the same three-step process of prepare, sign, and submit. However, we would be passing the additional parameter, `"condition"`.

Here's what the code to create a conditional escrow would look like:

```
'use strict';
const RippleAPI = require('ripple-lib').RippleAPI;
const sender = 'r41sFTd4rftxY1VCn5ZDDipb4KaV5VLFy2';
const secret = 'sptkAoSPzHq8mKLWrjU33EDj7v96u';
const options = {};
const release_date = new Date("2018-12-16T22:05:00Z");

const api = new RippleAPI({server: 'wss://s.altnet.rippletest.net:51233'});
api.connect().then(() => {
  console.log('Connected');
  return api.prepareEscrowCreation(sender, {
      "destination": "r42Qv8NwggeMWnpKcxMkx7qTtB23GYLHBX",
      "amount": '50',
      "allowExecuteAfter": release_date.toISOString(),
      "condition":
"A025802010BE1D1DE61FE69A9EE99689CB79820326BF6CA8A725F6631A0CE00A07B134DA81
0120"
  }, options);

}).then(prepared => {
  console.log("txJSON:", prepared.txJSON);
  const {signedTransaction} = api.sign(prepared.txJSON, secret);
  api.submit(signedTransaction).then(onSuccess,onFailure);
});

function onSuccess(message){
  console.log(message);
  console.log("Transaction Successfully Submitted.");
  disconnect();
}
```

```
function onFailure(message){
  console.log("Transaction Submission Failed.");
  console.log(message);
  disconnect();
}

function disconnect(){
  api.disconnect().then(()=> {
    console.log("Disconnected from test network.")
  });
}
```

Save this as `escrow_create.js`. Run it using the following command:

`./node_modules/.bin/babel-node escrow_create.js`

If everything goes well, you should be able to see the following output:

```
Febins-MacBook-Air:ConditionEscrow febinjohnjames$ ./node_modules/.bin/babel-node escrow_create.js
Connected
txJSON: {"TransactionType":"EscrowCreate","Account":"r41sFTd4rftxY1VCn5ZDDipb4KaV5VLFy2","Destination":"r42Qv8NwggeMWnpKcxMkx7qTtB23GYLHBX","
Amount":"50000000","Condition":"A025802010BE1D1DE61FE69A9EE99689CB79820326BF6CA8A725F6631A0CE00A07B134DA810120","FinishAfter":598313100,"Flag
s":2147483648,"LastLedgerSequence":15264588,"Fee":"12","Sequence":87}
{ resultCode: 'tesSUCCESS',
  resultMessage: 'The transaction was applied. Only final in a validated ledger.',
  engine_result: 'tesSUCCESS',
  engine_result_code: 0,
  engine_result_message: 'The transaction was applied. Only final in a validated ledger.',
  tx_blob: '12000122800000000024000000057201B00E8E84C202523A9888C614000000002FAF0806840000000000000000C73210247A93474AFDBA3962177E92624843403C99A8
E8B46B56430FFB4AEA9212DB69274473045022100EFB52360A996402260EBB4E7DBCAE8A68BAA97ED18C36BD5104D2DAAD2C2C8E402203E0B54BF8E026AD134A7177769323444
DBBE05F759331A69F55464E73708CC70701127A025802010BE1D1DE61FE69A9EE99689CB79820326BF6CA8A725F6631A0CE00A07B134DA81012081114EFD1CAC7F8FC974342DED
53BD4B1ABEDDEFD3A5E8314ECAC57766694E4FA7A00C5D1C1BEFC8E4D4CE1EA',
  tx_json:
   { Account: 'r41sFTd4rftxY1VCn5ZDDipb4KaV5VLFy2',
     Amount: '50000000',
     Condition: 'A025802010BE1D1DE61FE69A9EE99689CB79820326BF6CA8A725F6631A0CE00A07B134DA810120',
     Destination: 'r42Qv8NwggeMWnpKcxMkx7qTtB23GYLHBX',
     Fee: '12',
     FinishAfter: 598313100,
     Flags: 2147483648,
     LastLedgerSequence: 15264588,
     Sequence: 87,
     SigningPubKey: '0247A93474AFDBA3962177E92624843403C99A8E8B46B56430FFB4AEA9212DB692',
     TransactionType: 'EscrowCreate',
     TxnSignature: '3045022100EFB52360A996402260EBB4E7DBCAE8A68BAA97ED18C36BD5104D2DAAD2C2C8E402203E0B54BF8E026AD134A7177769323444DBBE05F7593
31A69F55464E73708CC70',
     hash: '8C811260FFB64D29AD5836D120B3868CA6B4E5B5E7D0F5750D96767B3ECB0886' } }
Transaction Successfully Submitted.
Disconnected from test network.
```

In order to release the escrow, we need to send both the condition and fulfillment. Here's the code to release the conditionally-held escrow:

```
'use strict';
const RippleAPI = require('ripple-lib').RippleAPI;

const sender = 'r41sFTd4rftxY1VCn5ZDDipb4KaV5VLFy2';
const secret = 'sptkAoSPzHq8mKLWrjU33EDj7v96u';
const options = {};
const release_date = new Date("2018-12-16T14:10:00Z");
```

```
const api = new RippleAPI({server: 'wss://s.altnet.rippletest.net:51233'});
api.connect().then(() => {
  console.log('Connected');
  return api.prepareEscrowExecution(sender, {
      "owner": sender,
      "escrowSequence": 87,
      "condition":
"A025802010BE1D1DE61FE69A9EE99689CB79820326BF6CA8A725F6631A0CE00A07B134DA81
0120",
      "fulfillment":
"A022802021EB4CB44AD71E3B2A23B4AAF6A546EA208960737C23F29F0645499968664404"
  }, options);

}).then(prepared => {
  console.log("txJSON:", prepared.txJSON);
  const {signedTransaction} = api.sign(prepared.txJSON, secret);
  api.submit(signedTransaction).then(onSuccess,onFailure);
});

function onSuccess(message){
  console.log(message);
  console.log("Transaction Successfully Submitted.");
  disconnect();
}

function onFailure(message){
  console.log("Transaction Submission Failed.");
  console.log(message);
  disconnect();
}

function disconnect(){
  api.disconnect().then(()=> {
    console.log("Disconnected from test network.");
  });
}
```

Save this as `escrow_release.js`. You can run it using the following command:

```
./node_modules/.bin/babel-node escrow_release.js
```

If everything goes well, you should be able to see the following output:

Febins-MacBook-Air:ConditionEscrow febinjohnjames$ ./node_modules/.bin/babel-node escrow_create.js
Connected
txJSON: {"TransactionType":"EscrowCreate","Account":"r41sFTd4rftxY1VCn5ZDDipb4KaV5VLFy2","Destination":"r42Qv8NwggeMWnpKcxMkx7qTtB23GYLHBX","
Amount":"50000000","Condition":"A025802010BE1D1DE61FE69A9EE99689CB79820326BF6CA8A725F6631A0CE00A07B134DA810120","FinishAfter":598313100,"Flag
s":2147483648,"LastLedgerSequence":15264588,"Fee":"12","Sequence":87}
{ resultCode: 'tesSUCCESS',
  resultMessage: 'The transaction was applied. Only final in a validated ledger.',
  engine_result: 'tesSUCCESS',
  engine_result_code: 0,
  engine_result_message: 'The transaction was applied. Only final in a validated ledger.',
  tx_blob: '12000122800000002400000057201B00E8EB4C202523A9888C614000000002FAF080684000000000000000000C73210247A93474AFDBA3962177E92624843403C99A8
E8B46B56430FFB4AEA9212DB69274473045022100EFB52360A996402260EBB4E7DBCAE8A68BAA97ED18C36BD5104D2DAAD2C2C8E402203E0B54BF8E026AD134A7177769323444
DBBE05F759331A69F55464E73708CC70701127A025802010BE1D1DE61FE69A9EE99689CB79820326BF6CA8A725F6631A0CE00A07B134DA81012081114EFD1CAC7F8FC974342DED
53BD4B1ABEDDEFD3A5E8314ECAC57766694E4FA7A00C5D1C1BEFC8E4D4CE1EA',
  tx_json:
   { Account: 'r41sFTd4rftxY1VCn5ZDDipb4KaV5VLFy2',
     Amount: '50000000',
     Condition: 'A025802010BE1D1DE61FE69A9EE99689CB79820326BF6CA8A725F6631A0CE00A07B134DA810120',
     Destination: 'r42Qv8NwggeMWnpKcxMkx7qTtB23GYLHBX',
     Fee: '12',
     FinishAfter: 598313100,
     Flags: 2147483648,
     LastLedgerSequence: 15264588,
     Sequence: 87,
     SigningPubKey: '0247A93474AFDBA3962177E92624843403C99A8E8B46B56430FFB4AEA9212DB692',
     TransactionType: 'EscrowCreate',
     TxnSignature: '3045022100EFB52360A996402260EBB4E7DBCAE8A68BAA97ED18C36BD5104D2DAAD2C2C8E402203E0B54BF8E026AD134A7177769323444DBBE05F7593
31A69F55464E73708CC70',
     hash: '8C811260FFB64D29AD5836D120B3868CA6B4E585E7D0F575DD96767B3ECB0886' } }
Transaction Successfully Submitted.
Disconnected from test network.

Once the transaction is confirmed by validators, the escrow will be released.

Let's now integrate this into our web app. The only change here is to the inputting of the condition and fulfillment. Here's what the JavaScript file should look like:

```javascript
const RippleAPI = require('ripple-lib').RippleAPI;

var api = new RippleAPI({server:'wss://s.altnet.rippletest.net:51233'});
var fetchBalance;
$('document').ready(function(){
  login();
  $('.progress').hide();
  $('#showCreateEscrowButton').click(function(){
      showcreateEscrowModal();
  });
  $('#logoutButton').click(function(){
      logout();
  });
  $("#loginButton").click(function(){
      storeCredentials();
  });
  $("#createEscrowButton").click(function(){
```

```
    createEscrow();
  });
  $("#releaseEscrowButton").click(function(){
    releaseEscrow();
  });
  $("#showReleaseEscrowButton").click(function(){
    showReleaseEscrowModal();
  });
});

function login(){
  if(!localStorage.getItem("loggedIn")){
    $('#loginModal').modal('show');
  } else{
    updateAccount();
  }
}

function logout(){
  localStorage.clear();
  clearInterval(fetchBalance);
  location.reload();
}

function updateAccount(){
  $('#rippleAddress').text(localStorage.getItem('rippleAddress'));
  updateBalance();
}

function storeCredentials(){
  localStorage.setItem("rippleAddress", $('#inputRippleAddress').val());
  localStorage.setItem("secret", $('#inputSecret').val());
  localStorage.setItem("loggedIn", true);
  $('#loginModal').modal('hide');
  updateAccount();
}

$("form").submit(function(e) {
  e.preventDefault();
});

function updateBalance(){
  api.connect().then(() => {
    const accountAddress = localStorage.getItem("rippleAddress");
    return api.getAccountInfo(accountAddress);
  }).then(info => {
    $('#balance').text("Account Balance : " + info.xrpBalance+ " XRP");
  }).then(() => {
```

```
      return api.disconnect();
   }).catch(console.error);
}

function showcreateEscrowModal(){
   $('#createEscrowModal').modal('show');
}

function showReleaseEscrowModal(){
   $('#releaseEscrowModal').modal('show');
}

function createEscrow(){
   $('.progress').show();
   const instructions = {};
   const sourceAddress = localStorage.getItem('rippleAddress');
   const sourceSecret = localStorage.getItem('secret');
   const releaseDateTime = new
Date($("#inputDate").val()+"T"+$("#inputTime").val()+"Z");
   const options = {};

   api.connect().then(() => {

   return api.prepareEscrowCreation(sourceAddress, {
       "destination": $("#inputDestinationAddress").val(),
       "amount": $("#inputAmount").val(),
       "allowExecuteAfter": releaseDateTime.toISOString(),
       "condition": $("#inputCondition").val()
   }, options).then(prepared => {
       $('.progress-bar').css('width', 40+'%').attr('aria-valuenow', 40);
       const {signedTransaction} = api.sign(prepared.txJSON,
sourceSecret);
       api.submit(signedTransaction).then(onSuccess,onFailure);
     });
   });
}

function releaseEscrow(){
     $('.progress').show();
     const instructions = {};
     const sourceAddress = localStorage.getItem('rippleAddress');
     const sourceSecret = localStorage.getItem('secret');
     const options = {};

     api.connect().then(() => {

     return api.prepareEscrowExecution(sourceAddress, {
         "owner": $("#inputOwnerAddress").val(),
```

```
            "escrowSequence": parseInt($("#inputSequence").val()),
            "condition": $("#inputReleaseCondition").val(),
            "fulfillment": $("#inputFulFillment").val()
        }, options).then(prepared => {
            $('.progress-bar').css('width', 40+'%').attr('aria-valuenow',
40);
            const {signedTransaction} = api.sign(prepared.txJSON,
sourceSecret);
            api.submit(signedTransaction).then(onSuccessRelease,onFailure);
        });
    });
  }

  function onSuccessRelease(message){
    $('.progress-bar').css('width', 100+'%').attr('aria-valuenow', 100);
    bootstrap_alert.success('Transaction Submitted Successfully');
    clear();
  }

  function onSuccess(message){
    console.log(message);
    $('.progress-bar').css('width', 100+'%').attr('aria-valuenow', 100);
    bootstrap_alert.success('Transaction Submitted Successfully');
    $('#escrowOutput').text("Created Escrow Sequence :
"+message['tx_json']['Sequence']);
    $('#balance').text("Fetching updated balance, please wait.");
    clear();
    setTimeout(updateBalance,6000);
  }

  function onFailure(message){
    console.log(message);
    $('.progress-bar').css('width', 100+'%').attr('aria-valuenow', 100);
    bootstrap_alert.danger('Transaction Submission Failed');
    clear();
  }

  function clear(){
    disconnect();
    $('#createEscrowModal').modal('hide');
    $('#releaseEscrowModal').modal('hide');
    $('.progress-bar').css('width', 0+'%').attr('aria-valuenow', 0);
    $(".progress").hide();
  }

  function disconnect(){
    api.disconnect().then(()=> {
    })
```

```
    }

  bootstrap_alert = function() {}

  bootstrap_alert.success = function(message) {
      $('#alert').html('<div role="alert" id="success-alert" class="alert
  alert-success"><p>'+message+'</p></div>');
      $("#success-alert").fadeTo(2000, 500).slideUp(500, function(){
          $("#success-alert").slideUp(500);
      });
    }
  bootstrap_alert.danger = function(message) {
      $('#alert').html('<div role="alert" id="danger-alert" class="alert
  alert-danger"><p>'+message+'</p></div>');
      $("#danger-alert").fadeTo(2000, 500).slideUp(500, function(){
      $("#danger-alert").slideUp(500);
  });
  });
  }
```

Save this file as `app.js`. Let's `browserify` it using the following command:

```
browserify app.js -o bundle.js
```

Here's what the file should look like:

```
<!DOCTYPE html>
<html>
<title> Condition Escrow </title>
<head>
  <link rel="stylesheet" href="css/bootstrap.min.css">
</head>
<body>

<nav class="navbar navbar-expand-lg navbar-dark bg-dark">
  <a class="navbar-brand" href="#">Condition Escrow</a>
</nav>

<br/><br/><br/>

<center>
  <p class="lead">Ripple Address : <span id="rippleAddress"> </span> </p>
  <p id="balance"> Please wait, fetching account details...</p>
  <button id="showCreateEscrowButton" class="btn btn-primary">Create Time-
Held Escrow</button>
    <button id="showReleaseEscrowButton" class="btn btn-primary">Release
Escrow</button>

    <button id="logoutButton" class="btn btn-primary">Logout</button>
```

```
      <br/>
      <br/>
      <br/>
      <div id="escrowOutput"> </div>
      <div id="alert" style="width:30%"></div>
</center>

<div class="modal fade" id="loginModal" tabindex="-1" role="dialog" aria-
labelledby="loginModalLabel" aria-hidden="true">
   <div class="modal-dialog" role="document">
      <div class="modal-content">
         <div class="modal-header">
            <h5 class="modal-title" id="loginModalLabel">Login</h5>
            <button type="button" class="close" data-dismiss="modal" aria-
label="Close">
               <span aria-hidden="true">&times;</span>
            </button>
         </div>
         <div class="modal-body">
            <form>
            <div class="form-group">
               <label for="inputRippleAddress">Ripple Address</label>
               <input type="text" class="form-control" id="inputRippleAddress"
aria-describedby="rippleAddressHelp" placeholder="Enter Ripple Address">
            </div>
            <div class="form-group">
               <label for="inputSecret">Secret</label>
               <input type="password" class="form-control" id="inputSecret"
placeholder="Secret">
            </div>

            <button id="loginButton" class="btn btn-primary">Login</button>
         </form>
         </div>


      </div>
   </div>
</div>

<div class="modal fade" id="createEscrowModal" tabindex="-1" role="dialog"
aria-labelledby="createEscrowModalLabel" aria-hidden="true">
   <div class="modal-dialog" role="document">
      <div class="modal-content">
         <div class="modal-header">
            <h5 class="modal-title" id="createEscrowModalLabel">Create Escrow
</h5>
            <button type="button" class="close" data-dismiss="modal" aria-
label="Close">
```

```
          <span aria-hidden="true">&times;</span>
        </button>
      </div>
      <div class="modal-body">
        <form>
        <div class="form-group">
          <label for="inputDestinationAddress">Destination</label>
          <input type="text" class="form-control"
id="inputDestinationAddress" aria-describedby="inputDestinationAddressHelp"
placeholder="Destination Address">
        </div>
          <div class="form-group">
            <label for="inputCondition">Condition</label>
            <input type="text" class="form-control" id="inputCondition"
aria-describedby="inputConditionHelp" placeholder="Condition">
          </div>
        <div class="form-group">
          <label for="inputAmount">Amount</label>
          <input type="number" class="form-control" id="inputAmount"
placeholder="Amount">
        </div>
        <div class="form-group">
          <label for="inputDate">Release Date (UTC)</label>
          <input type="date" class="form-control" id="inputDate"
placeholder="Date">
        </div>
          <div class="form-group">
            <label for="inputTime">Release Time (UTC)</label>
            <input type="time" class="form-control" id="inputTime"
placeholder="Time">
          </div>

        <button id="createEscrowButton" class="btn btn-primary">Create
Escrow</button>
        <br/> <br/>
        <div class="progress">
        <div class="progress-bar progress-bar-striped bg-info"
role="progressbar" style="width: 0%" aria-valuenow="0" aria-valuemin="0"
aria-valuemax="100"></div>
        </div>
      </form>
      </div>

    </div>
  </div>
</div>

<div class="modal fade" id="releaseEscrowModal" tabindex="-1" role="dialog"
```

```
aria-labelledby="releaseEscrowModalLabel" aria-hidden="true">
  <div class="modal-dialog" role="document">
    <div class="modal-content">
      <div class="modal-header">
        <h5 class="modal-title" id="releaseEscrowModalLabel">Release Escrow
</h5>
        <button type="button" class="close" data-dismiss="modal" aria-
label="Close">
          <span aria-hidden="true">&times;</span>
        </button>
      </div>
      <div class="modal-body">
        <form>
        <div class="form-group">
          <label for="inputOwnerAddress">Owner</label>
          <input type="text" class="form-control" id="inputOwnerAddress"
aria-describedby="inputOwnerAddressHelp" placeholder="Owner Address">
        </div>
        <div class="form-group">
          <label for="inputSequence">Sequence</label>
          <input type="number" class="form-control" id="inputSequence"
placeholder="Sequence">
        </div>
          <div class="form-group">
            <label for="inputReleaseCondition">Condition</label>
            <input type="text" class="form-control"
id="inputReleaseCondition" aria-describedby="inputReleaseConditionHelp"
placeholder="Condition">
          </div>
            <div class="form-group">
              <label for="inputFulFillment">Fulfillment</label>
              <input type="text" class="form-control" id="inputFulFillment"
aria-describedby="inputFulFillmentHelp" placeholder="Fulfillment">
            </div>

        <button id="releaseEscrowButton" class="btn btn-primary">Release
Escrow</button>
        <br/> <br/>
        <div class="progress">
        <div class="progress-bar progress-bar-striped bg-info"
role="progressbar" style="width: 0%" aria-valuenow="0" aria-valuemin="0"
aria-valuemax="100"></div>
        </div>
      </form>
      </div>

    </div>
  </div>
```

```
</div>

</body>

<script src="js/jquery.min.js"></script>
<script src="js/bootstrap.min.js"></script>
<script src="js/bundle.js"></script>
</html>
```

Save the file as `escrow_create.html`. Now you can run it on the browser and you should be able to see a screen similar to the following one to create the conditionally-held escrow:

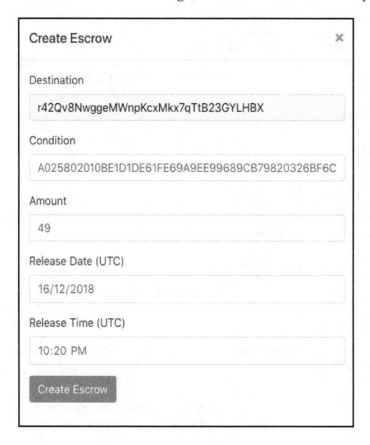

The release escrow form should be similar to the following screenshot:

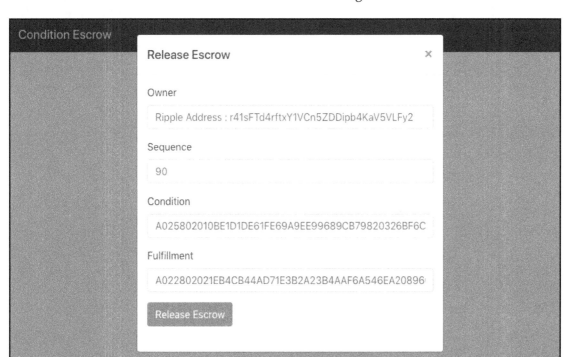

Great job! You've completed building an app that allows users to create their own conditionally-held escrows.

Important things you must remember

Following are some important points that you must when on Ripple:

- Most transactions on Ripple follow the three-step process of preparing the transaction, signing it, and submitting it.
- Transactions are applied only when validators approve the transaction.
- When a check is created on Ripple, no money is deducted until it's cashed out.
- Escrow in Ripple doesn't support issues currencies. It only supports XRP.

- Time-held escrows in Ripple can be released by anyone only after the release time is passed. However, the money is released only to the destination account specified by the sender.
- A conditionally-held escrow needs the condition and fulfillment to be passed in order to release the locked funds.

Summary

In this chapter, we learned the following things:

- How to cash a check
- How to create and release a time-held escrow
- How to create and release a conditionally-held escrow
- How to build a user interface by integrating Ripple APIs into a web app

Now, that you're familiar with Ripple APIs, please have a look at the Ripple Developer Docs. It would give you access to more functionalities. You'll also be updated when new features are added. You can also follow the Ripple community on Reddit.

Other Books You May Enjoy

If you enjoyed this book, you may be interested in these other books by Packt:

Tokenomics

Sean Au

ISBN: 9781789136326

- The background of ICOs and how they came to be
- The difference between a coin and a token, a utility and a security, and all the other acronyms you're likely to ever encounter
- How these ICOs raised enormous sums of money
- Tokenomics: structuring the token with creativity
- Why it's important to play nicely with the regulators
- A sneak peak into the future of ICOs from leaders in the industry

Blockchain Quick Reference
Brenn Hill

ISBN: 9781788995788

- Understand how blockchain architecture components work
- Acquaint yourself with cryptography and the mechanics behind blockchain
- Apply consensus protocol to determine the business sustainability
- Understand what ICOs and crypto-mining are and how they work
- Create cryptocurrency wallets and coins for transaction mechanisms
- Understand the use of Ethereum for smart contract and App development

Leave a review - let other readers know what you think

Please share your thoughts on this book with others by leaving a review on the site that you bought it from. If you purchased the book from Amazon, please leave us an honest review on this book's Amazon page. This is vital so that other potential readers can see and use your unbiased opinion to make purchasing decisions, we can understand what our customers think about our products, and our authors can see your feedback on the title that they have worked with Packt to create. It will only take a few minutes of your time, but is valuable to other potential customers, our authors, and Packt. Thank you!

Index

X

xCurrent
  about 50
  FX ticker 51

  messenger 50
  validator 50
  working 51
XRP
  exchanging, for cryptocurrencies 38, 40, 41